School Days

The Little Red Hen
found some wheat.
She called the cat
She called the dog
She called the pig

Sweet Memories

1st Printing – December 1998
2nd Printing – March 1999
3rd Printing – August 2000

Printed in Canada by
The Aylmer Express, Aylmer, Ontario, Canada

School Days
Sweet Memories

FOREWORD

My favourite story, when I started to read, was the story of the Little Red Hen. It and many more came from the Ontario Readers Primer, and the Ontario Readers First and Second books. These readers were used in all elementary schools in Ontario in those days.

Now, in my twilight years, I have a great desire to share these stories with the present young generation. I could only remember some of the verses and stories. I decided to search the Libraries both in London and in Strathroy for copies of the readers. But to no avail. Finally, I advertised in the Age Dispatch that if anyone had copies of these readers, I would be pleased to borrow them. I received answers from two people: Mrs. Orville Sutherland of Mt. Brydges and Ms. Mary Carmichael of Ilderton who were kind enough to lend me them.

The question that harassed me was how to preserve these children's gems. It was through the help of Mr. Robert Engels, the Poplar Hill Printer, that I was able to overcome the problem. First, I had to get permission to publish the contents of these readers so that today's children could also enjoy them. Mr. Mark Robinson of the Publications Ontario Copyright Unit gave us permission to use all or parts of these readers in a single volume. I must thank these people for assisting me in accomplishing something that has always been dear to my heart.

All profits from the sale of this book are being donated to providing good water in Africa.

MASON FLETCHER

SCHOOL DAYS

"School days, school days
Good old golden rule days,
Reading, writing, and arithmetic
Taught to the tune of the hickory stick"

We didn't rule the roost at school
We sat in our own seat; did what the teacher said,
Learned our reading, writing and arithmetic
And it served us well in the years ahead.

Our luxuries were few, our food was good
No junk food to tempt us, or bubble gum,
Our old privy was always "air conditioned"
Sometimes I almost froze my bum.

Maybe I'm slipping into 2nd childhood
By the computers of today I'm not very clever,
But if we don't preserve these old country readers
They will be lost, forgotten and gone forever.

MASON FLETCHER

SENIORS

Come along with me down memories lane
When our hearts were young and gay,
Our little bare feet and our sunburnt nose
And we were always ready and willing to play.

I don't remember much of my childhood
A toy car, tinker toys, crayons, and a stool,
The greatest change I ever had in my life
Was the day I left home and started to school.

We had a young and good lookin' teacher
And I was lookin' away back then,
She completely stole my little heart away
When she told me the story of the little red hen.

So let us wander back to our childhood days
And through the pages of time have a look,
Sweet memories I'm sure will pop into your head
As we search through an old readers book.

MASON

THE ONTARIO READERS

PRIMER

AUTHORIZED BY
THE MINISTER OF EDUCATION

PRICE 4 CENTS

TORONTO
THE T. EATON CO LIMITED
3-'28

The Little Red Hen
found some wheat.
She called the cat.
She called the dog.
She called the pig.

"Who will help me plant
      the wheat?"
"Not I," said the cat.
"Not I," said the dog.
"Not I," said the pig.
"Then I will plant
      the wheat,"
Said the Little Red Hen.
    And she did.

The wheat grew up.
The Little Red Hen said,
"Who will help me cut
the wheat?"
"Not I," said the cat.
"Not I," said the dog.
"Not I," said the pig.
"Then I will cut the wheat,"
Said the Little Red Hen.
And she did.

The Little Red Hen said,
"Who will help me grind
the wheat?"
"Not I," said the cat.
"Not I," said the dog.
"Not I," said the pig.
"Then I will grind the wheat,"
Said the Little Red Hen.
And she did!

The Little Red Hen said,
"Who will help me make
the bread?"
"Not I," said the cat.
"Not I," said the dog.
"Not I," said the pig.
"Then I will make the bread,"
Said the Little Red Hen.
And she did.

The Little Red Hen said,
"Who will help me bake
the bread?"
"Not I," said the cat.
"Not I," said the dog.
"Not I," said the pig.
"Then I will bake the bread,"
Said the Little Red Hen.
And she did.

The Little Red Hen said,
"Who will help me eat
the bread?"
"I will," said the cat.
"I will," said the dog.
"I will," said the pig.

The Little Red Hen said,
"You would not plant
the wheat.
You would not cut
the wheat.
You would not grind
the wheat.
You would not bake
the bread.
You shall not eat
the bread.
My little chicks shall eat
the bread."
And they did.

red dog bake little

red   dog   bake   little

you will some found

you   will   some   found

Who called the cat?

Who   called   the   cat?

Who will help the hen?

Who   will   help   the   hen?

Will you get the flour?

Will   you   get   the   flour?

Did the chicks eat bread?

Did   the   chicks   eat   bread?

I see I can He has

I see I can He has

Do you It is I am

Do you It is I am

I can see the pig.

I can see the pig.

He has some wheat.

He has some wheat.

It is my wheat.

It is my wheat.

Who am I? Do you see?

Who am I? Do you see?

This little pig went to market.
This little pig stayed at home.
This little pig had roast beef.
This little pig had none.
This little pig said,
    "Wee, wee,"
All the way home.

Rain, rain, go away,
Come again some other day,
Little Tommy wants to play.
Rain, rain, go away.

HUMPTY DUMPTY

Humpty Dumpty sat on the wall,
Humpty Dumpty had a great fall.
    All the King's horses,
    And all the King's men,
Couldn't pick Humpty Dumpty
    up again.

———

Little Jack Horner sat in a corner,
    Eating Christmas pie;
    He put in his thumb
    And pulled out a plum,
And said, "What a good boy am I."

JACK AND JILL

Jack and Jill
Went up the hill
To get a pail of water;
   Jack fell down
    And broke his crown,

               And
               Jill
                came
                tumbling
                 after.

There were two robins,
In an old tree top.
One was called Pip,
The other called Pop.

Fly away, Pip.
Fly away, Pop.
   Come back, Pip.
   Come back, Pop.

THE WIND

Who has seen the wind?
  Neither you nor I;
But when the leaves hang
    trembling,
  The wind is passing by.

Who has seen the wind?
  Neither I nor you;
But when the trees bow down
    their heads,
  The wind is passing through.

CHRISTINA ROSSETTI

HUSH A BYE

Hush a bye baby
    On the tree top,
When the wind blows,
    The cradle will rock.

When the bough breaks,
    The cradle will fall,
Down tumbles baby,
    Bough, cradle, and all.

Little Boy Blue,
Come blow your horn.
The sheep are in the meadow,
The cows are in the corn.
Where is the little boy
Who looks after the sheep?
He is under the haystack,
Fast asleep.

This is Little Boy Blue.
He does not see the sheep
and the cows.
Where are the sheep?
Where are the cows?
Come, Little Boy Blue,
Wake up and blow your horn.

THE HORN

Once upon a time there was a horn.

It lived in a toy shop.

One day it said, "I will go and play with Little Boy Blue."

It went out of the shop and down the road.   It met a drum.

"Good morning," said the drum. "Where are you going?"

"I am going to play with Little Boy Blue.   Will you come too?" said the horn.

"Yes, I will," said the drum. So the horn and the drum went to find Little Boy Blue.

Soon they met a gun. "Where are you going?" said the gun. "To play with Little Boy Blue," said the horn and the drum. " Will you come too?"

"Yes, I will," said the gun.

So the horn and the drum and the gun went to find Little Boy Blue. Boy Blue was under the haystack, fast asleep.

" Who will wake him?" said the horn.

"I will," said the drum.

"I will," said the gun.

"No, I will," said the horn; and it blew so loudly that up jumped Little Boy Blue.

And the horn and the drum and the gun played with him all day.

LITTLE BO-PEEP

Little Bo-Peep
Has lost her sheep,
  And cannot tell
  Where to find them.
Leave them alone,
And they will come
     home,
  And bring their tails
Behind them.

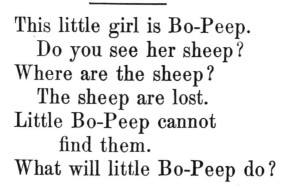

This little girl is Bo-Peep.
  Do you see her sheep?
Where are the sheep?
  The sheep are lost.
Little Bo-Peep cannot
  find them.
What will little Bo-Peep do?

OUR FLAG

This is our flag.
It is the Union Jack.
The flag is red, white, and blue.
The red says, "Be brave!"
The white says, "Be pure!"
The blue says, "Be true!"
Our soldiers fought
for this flag in the Great War.

*This was our old flag which our
grandfathers fought for.
Now we have our own flag with the maple leaf
that was approved October 22/1964.*

FIVE LITTLE BIRDS

We are little birds.
One, two, three, four, five.
We are five little birds.
Five little birds can fly.
Five little birds can sing.
One little bird sings,
   "How do you do?"
And one little bird sings,
   "I like you."

And one little bird sings,
   "A crust, if you please."
And one little bird sings,
   "I like cheese."
And one little bird sings,
   "South we must fly."
So one, two, three, four, five
   Little birds sang,
      "Good-bye, good-bye."

One, two, three, four little ducks,
and two little chickens.

One little chicken peeps,
"How do you do?"

And one little duck quacks,
"I'll chase you!"

Another little duck quacks,
"Hear me talk!"

Another little duck quacks,
"See me walk!"

Another little duck quacks,
"Watch me swim!"

And one little chicken peeps,
"Don't go in!"

See the people running!
Why are they running?
They are shouting, too.
What are they shouting?
Oh, hear the bells ringing!
What is the matter?
Why, don't you know? It is a fire!
Look! There it is, down there!
Here comes the fire engine.
How fast the horses go!
Let us go, too.

WHO AM I?

You may hear me call,
    but no one has ever seen me.
I fly kites for boys.
I play with the leaves.
I scatter the seeds of plants.
I rock the bird in her nest.
I move clouds across the sky.
I toss ships on the sea.
I am now hot, now cold.
I am now strong, now weak.
Who am I?

THE HORSE AND THE GOOSE

This is a horse and this is a goose.
The horse looks at the goose.
The goose looks at the horse.
The goose speaks to the horse.
This is what she says:

    "I am better than you.

    I can walk on the ground like
        you.

    I can fly in the air like a bird.

    I can swim in the water like a
        fish.

    I am as good as a horse.

    I am as good as a bird.

    I am as good as a fish."

This is what the horse says
      to the goose:
"It is true!---
    You can walk on the ground.
    You can fly in the air.
    You can swim in the water.
But---
    You cannot walk as well as a
       horse.
    You cannot fly as well as a bird.
    You cannot swim as well as a
       fish.
      I cannot fly in the air.
      I cannot swim in the water.
But---
    I can walk well upon the ground.
    And I would rather do one thing
    well than be a goose in more
    ways than one!"

Translated from First Lessons
in French—Baguley
By special permission of
Edward Arnold

THE LITTLE PLANT

In the heart of a seed,
   Buried deep, so deep,
A dear little plant
   Lay fast asleep.

"Wake!" said the sunshine,
   "And creep to the light."
"Wake!" said the voice
   Of the raindrops bright.

The little plant heard,
   And it rose to see
What the wonderful world
   Outside might be.

K. L. Brown

MY LITTLE GARDEN

I have a little garden,
   And every summer day
I dig it well, and rake it well,
   And pull the weeds away.

I have a little garden,
   And every summer night
I water all the pretty flowers,
   And watch them with delight.

. . . .

In my little garden
   I have a little walk;
I take my sisters by the hand,
   And there we go and talk.

Busy bees come humming by,
   To gather honey sweet;
And singing birds look in to see
   What they can get to eat.

. . . .

AGNES VEITCH

"This stocking is full," said
     Santa Claus—
  "As full as it can be."
A mouse sat licking his little paws,
Not far from the Christmas tree.

  He saw and heard old
     Santa Claus,
Then he ran across the floor

And said, "Just let me try, because
I'm sure I can put in more."

Old Santa Claus laughed and shook his head,
"You cannot do it, I know;"
But mousie gnawed and gnawed and gnawed,
And put a hole in the toe.

THE CHILD AND THE STAR

Bright little star,
Shining afar,
Tell me, I pray,
What means Christmas Day?

Christmas, my child,
Is a song from above,
The sweet, happy song
Of God's great love.

THE UMBRELLA

The rain is raining all around,
It falls on field and tree,
It rains on the umbrellas here,
And on the ships at sea.

It is raining all around.
Who has an umbrella?

"I have," said the lark;
And he flew under a leaf.

"I have," said the spider;
And he crept under a stone.

"I have," said the bee;
And he went into a flower bell.

"I don't want one," said the goose;
And she ran out into the rain.

OLD MOTHER HUBBARD

Old Mother Hubbard
Went to the cupboard
　　To get her poor dog a bone;
But when she got there,
The cupboard was bare,
　　And so the poor dog had none.

She went to the hatter's
　　To buy him a hat;
But when she came back,
　　He was feeding the cat.

She went to the tailor's
   To buy him a coat;
But when she came back,
   He was riding a goat.

The dame made a curtsy,
   The dog made a bow;
The dame said, "Your servant,"
   The dog said, "Bow-wow."

WISHES

Said the first little chicken,
With a sad little sigh,
"I wish I could find
A little fat fly."

Said the next little chicken,
With an odd little shrug,
"I wish I could find
A fat little bug."

Said the third little chicken,
With a sharp little squeak,
"I wish I could feel
Some corn in my beak."

Said the fourth little chicken,
With a small sigh of grief,
"I wish I could find
A fat worm on a leaf."

"See here," said the mother,
From the green garden patch,
"If you want things to eat,
Just come here and scratch."

The cow has a horn, and the fish
 has a gill;
The horse has a hoof, and the duck
 has a bill;
The cat has a paw, and the dog
 has a tail;
And the bird has a wing that on high
 it may sail.

THE HOUSE

There once was a mouse
Who lived in a shoe,
And a snug little house
He made of it, too;
    He had a front door
    To take in the cheese,
    And a hole in the toe
    To slip out, if you please.

———

    There are roses
        that grow on a vine,
    There are roses
        that grow on a tree,
    But my little Rose
        grows on ten little toes,
And she is the rose for me.

Well, old doggie.   I have come
            to talk to you.
Shake hands.   Give me your paw.
Say, "How do you do?"
Why can't you talk to me?
When I tell you to talk,
            you only bark.
But you are a good doggie.
I like your white nose.
My kitty has a white nose, too.
But why is your nose so cold?
This is my little kitty.
Why can't you talk to us?

THE LITTLE RAINDROPS

Oh! Where do you come from,
You little drops of rain,
Pitter, patter, pitter, patter,
Down the window-pane?

Tell me, little raindrops,
Is that the way you play,
Pitter, patter, pitter, patter,
All the rainy day?

The little raindrops cannot speak,
But "pitter, patter, pat,"
Means, "we can play on this side,
Why can't you play on that?"

Mrs. Hawkshaw

THE RAIN

It is raining!   It is raining!
 Who likes the rain?
The little duck laughs and says,
 "I--I love the rain!"

The little girl says,
 "I do not like the rain.
The rain spoils my dress."
 See the little girl
  under her umbrella.
 She runs as fast as she can
  to the house.

"I like the rain!"
　says the little boy.
He is running to school.
He has not an umbrella,
　but he has a big coat.
He likes water.　He likes rain.
He is like the little duck,
　who laughs and says,
"I love the rain!"

Translated from First Lessons
in French—Baguley
By special permission of
Edward Arnold

THE CLEVER DOG

One day a little dog was playing
on the road, when a sharp nail ran
into his paw.

His master was a doctor's son,
and he took the dog to his father.

The doctor drew the nail out,
washed the paw, and tied it up.

The next day the little dog
was playing with a big one.

A sharp stick ran into the paw
of the big dog, and hurt him so
that he began to howl.

The little dog coaxed the big one
to go with him at once to the doctor
who had helped him the day before.

The good doctor was able to help
the big dog, too.

Was he not a clever little dog?

THE WISE FOX

One day a lion sat at the door of
his cave. He saw a dog passing by.

"Come in, my friend, and visit
me for a while," he said.
The dog was proud to have the lion
speak to him.

He went in, but never came out.
Soon after, a bear passed that way.
The lion said to him, "Come in and
make me a little visit, Mr. Bear."

The bear went in, but never
came out.

A wolf was walking by, and the
lion asked him in for a visit.

The wolf said, "Thank you, Sir Lion,
I shall be pleased to visit you."

But he never came out.
Many beasts went into the cave,
but none ever came out.

One day a fox went to see the lion.
"Are you at home, old lion?" he said.
"Come in, come in," said the lion.

The fox looked down on the
ground, and saw some tracks on
the sand.

"Come in, come in," called the lion.
"Why do you not come in?   I
cannot go out to see you.   Do
walk in!"

"No, thank you," said the fox.
"I think I will not come in to-day.
I see some tracks on the sand.
They all go into the cave. I see no
tracks coming out.   I think I will
walk away.   Good-day, old lion!"

JACK AND TOM
(A Dialogue)

When did you get the dog, Jack?
I got him to-day, Tom.
To-day is my birthday.
Who gave you the dog?
Father gave him to me.
How old are you, Jack?
I am seven, Tom.
Do you go to school?
Oh, yes! I go to school.
Do you like school?
Yes, I like to go to school.
Can you read, Jack?
I can read a little, Tom.

What class are you in?
I am in the Primer.
Is that your Primer in your bag?
Yes, this is my book.
Look! I can read
>Little Jack Horner,
>Little Boy Blue, and
>Little Bo-Peep.

THE LITTLE ROSEBUSH

Good-morning, little rosebush,
>I pray thee, tell me true,
To be as sweet as a sweet red rose
>What must a body do?

To be as sweet as a sweet red rose,
>A little girl like you
Just grows, and grows, and grows,
>>and grows,
>And that's what she must do.

JOEL STACY

THE TEA-PARTY

Let us have a tea-party, Polly!
Yes, that will be lovely;
   Whom shall we ask, Molly?
All your dolls, and all my dolls,
   and the little girl next door.
Very well, and what shall we have
   to drink?
I like tea the best, and so do
   the dollies, Polly.
But I like coffee the best;
   do let us have coffee, Molly.
No, I don't like coffee so much
   as tea.

But I like it ever so much better;
   can't we have coffee this time?
All right! We will have coffee
   this time, if you like.
That will be lovely! Shall I go and
   ask the little girl next door?
Yes, please do; and I will set
   the table.
So all the dolls, and Molly and Polly
   had a lovely tea-party together.

LULLABY

Sleep, my baby, sleep and rest
In your cosy little nest;
Into dreamland gently go,
While I sing so sweet and low,
    Lullaby, lullaby,
    Lullaby, my baby.

THE THREE BEARS

One day little Goldie-Locks went
to the woods to pick flowers.
She walked on and on.

At last she saw a little house.
It was the home of three bears.
Father Bear was a great big bear.
Mother Bear was a middle-sized one.
Baby Bear was a little wee bear.

The bears had gone for a walk.
Goldie-Locks saw the door was open,
so she walked in to the kitchen.

On the table she saw three bowls

of soup—a big bowl, a middle-sized bowl, and a little wee bowl.

Goldie-Locks tasted the soup in the big bowl.   But it was too hot.

She tasted the soup in the middle-sized bowl.   But it was too cool.

The soup in the little wee bowl was just right, and she took it all.

Goldie-Locks saw three chairs. The first was a great big chair. The second was a middle-sized one. The third was a little wee chair.

Goldie-Locks sat in the great

big chair.   But it was too high.

She sat in the middle-size
chair.   But it was too wide.

So she sat in the little
wee chair.   But the little
wee chair broke, and down she fell.

She jumped up and ran upstairs.
There she found three beds—
a big bed, a middle-sized bed,
and a little wee bed.

She lay down on the big bed.
But it was too hard.

She lay down on the middle-sized
bed.   But it was too soft.

So she tried the little wee bed.
It was just right, and she soon
fell fast asleep.

Father Bear, Mother Bear, and
Baby Bear came home very hungry.
They went at once to get their soup.

Father Bear growled, "Some one
has been tasting my soup!"

Mother Bear cried out, "Some
one has been tasting my soup!"

Then Baby Bear said, in his
little wee voice, "Some one
has been tasting my soup, and
it is all gone!"

Then the three bears wanted to
sit down and rest.

Father Bear growled, "Some one
has been sitting in my chair!"

Mother Bear cried out, "Some
one has been sitting in my chair!"

Baby Bear said, "Some one
has been sitting in my chair,
and has broken it!"

The three bears were very angry.
Then they went upstairs to bed.

"Some one has been lying on

my bed!" growled Father Bear.

"Some one has been lying on my bed!" cried out Mother Bear.

"Some one is lying in my bed now, and she is fast asleep!" called out Baby Bear.

Goldie-Locks woke up, and saw the three bears.

They gave her a great fright.

She jumped out of the window, and ran home as fast as she could.

LITTLE STAR

Good-night, little star!
  I must go to my bed,
And leave you to shine,
  While I lay down my head..

Oh, soundly I'll sleep,
  Till the sweet morning light;
Then you will be fading,
  But I shall be bright.

Yes, while I'm asleep,
  You will play in the sky;
And when I awake,
  You will close your bright eye.

—Author unknown

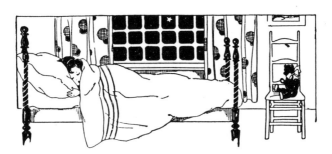

THE THREE LITTLE PIGS

Mother Pig had three little pigs.
She had not food for them all to eat.

She said to the first little pig,
"You must go away, and make a
house of your own."

So the first little pig left home.
He met a man with some straw.

"Good-morning, Mr. Man," said
the little pig.   "Please give me
that straw to make me a house."

So the man gave him the straw.
Then the little pig made a house.

The next day Mr. Wolf came along.

He rapped at the door, and said,
"Little Pig, Little Pig, let me in,
let me in!"

"No, no, my good sir, you shall
never come in!"

"Then I'll huff and I'll puff,
and I'll blow your house in!"

So he huffed and he puffed, and
he blew the house in.   Then he
ate up the poor little pig.

The second little pig left home.
He met a man with a bundle of
sticks.

"Please Mr. Man, give me those
sticks to make me a house."

So the man gave him the sticks.
Then the little pig made a house.
The next day Mr. Wolf came along.

He rapped at the door, and said,

"Little Pig, Little Pig, let me in,
let me in!"

"No, no, my good sir, you shall
never come in!"

"Then I'll huff and I'll puff,
and I'll blow your house in!"

So he huffed and he puffed, and
he blew the house in. Then he
ate up the poor little pig.

The third little pig left home.
He met a man with some bricks.
"Good-morning, Mr. Man. Please
give me those bricks to make me
a house."

So the man gave him the bricks.
Then the little pig made a house.
The next day Mr. Wolf came along.

He rapped at the door, and said,
"Little Pig, Little Pig, let me in,
let me in!"

"No, no, my good sir, you shall
never come in!"

"Then I'll huff and I'll puff,
and I'll blow your house in!"

So he huffed and he puffed, and
he puffed and he huffed.   But he
could not blow the house in.
The bricks were too strong.

Then Mr. Wolf said, "I will jump
up on the roof.   I will jump down
the chimney, and eat you up!"

Then the little pig took a big
kettle. He hung it over the hot fire.
He filled it full of boiling water.

Then Mr. Wolf jumped into the
chimney. He fell down, down, down,
plump into the kettle of hot water!

That was the end of Mr. Wolf.

—English Nursery Tale

ONE THING AT A TIME

Work while you work,
  Play while you play,
That is the way
  To be happy and gay.

Whatever you do,
  Do with your might.
Things done by halves
  Are never done right.

One thing at a time,
  And that done well,
Is the best of all rules,
  As many can tell.

———

If you try and try and try,
And do not pout or cry,
You will find by and by
It is best to try and try.

THE CAT AND THE BIRD

"Good-morning, little Bird," said Pussy.

"Good-morning, Pussy," said the little Bird.

"Will you fly down to me, little Bird?" said Pussy.

"Why should I fly down to you?" said the little Bird.

"I like a little Bird for my breakfast," said Pussy.

"A little Bird does not like to be a breakfast for a Pussy," said the Bird, and away he flew.

THE DUCKS AND THE FROGS

The ducks were out on the river diving for food. Some frogs saw them.

"What funny things ducks are!" said one frog. "Yes, they have only two legs," said another frog.

"Good-day, Mrs. Duck," said another. "Is your home in the water?"

"No, indeed!" said Mrs. Duck. "Our home is at the farm. We have a house there. Our Mistress made it for us."

"Why did she make you a house?"
said the frog. "She never made
one for us."

"Why, we lay eggs for her," said
Mrs. Duck.

"Well, we lay eggs, too," said the
frog.

"You lay your eggs in the water,"
said Mrs. Duck, "but we lay ours in
our house. Men like to eat our
eggs, but they do not care for
yours."

"What funny things men are!"
said the frog, as the duck swam
away.

"How lucky for us that they are!"
said another frog, as he dived from
the bank.

THE DOG IN THE MANGER

One day in summer a big dog went into a stable.

He saw a manger full of soft hay. He crept into it and fell asleep.

An ox who had been working hard came into the stable. He was tired and hungry. He went to the manger to eat, but the dog growled at him.

"Do you want to eat the hay?" asked the ox.

"No," growled the dog. "I can't
eat hay."

"Then let me eat it," said the ox.

"I will not," said the dog.

"What a mean dog you are!"
said the ox. "You can't eat it, and
I can; yet you will not let me eat it."

WHITE SHEEP

White sheep, white sheep,
  On a blue hill,
When the wind stops,
  You all stand still.

When the wind blows,
  You walk away slow.
White sheep, white sheep,
  Where do you go?

THE STORY OF HENNY PENNY

Henny Penny was walking in a
garden.   A cherry fell
on her head with a thud.
"The sky is falling,"
said Henny Penny. "I
must run and tell the King."

As she ran, she met a Rooster,
who said,   "Where are you going,
Henny Penny?"
And she cried, "Oh,
Rooster Pooster!   the
sky is falling, and I
am going to tell the King."

"I will go, too," said Rooster
Pooster.

So they ran and ran
till they met a Turkey.
"Oh, Turkey Lurkey!"

said they, "the sky is falling, and we are going to tell the King."

"I will go with you," said Turkey Lurkey.

So they ran and ran till they met a Fox.

"Oh, Fox Lox!" said they, "the sky is falling, and we are going to tell the King."

And the Fox said, "Come with me, Henny Penny, Rooster Pooster, and Turkey Lurkey. I will show you the way to the King's house."

But they said, "Oh, no, Fox Lox! we know you."

So they ran and ran, but they never found the King's house.

And the King never knew the sky was falling.

THE GREEDY MAN

There was once
a man who had a
góose. She laid
an egg every day.
One day she laid
a golden egg.

The man went
to town and sold

the egg.   Next day the goose laid
another golden egg.

"Wife," said the man, "we shall
not be poor any more."

Every day he found a golden egg
and sold it.   Soon he was not content with this.

"Wife," said he, "I shall kill this
goose and get all the eggs at once."

So he killed her, but he found no
golden eggs!

ROBIN REDBREAST

It was early in the morning, and Robin sat on the tree top.

"Cheer-up, cheer-up! cheer-up, cheer-up!" he sang.

The old cat heard him, and crept under the tree.   She called softly,

"Robin, Robin Redbreast,
Singing on the bough,
Come and get your breakfast,
I will feed you now."

"Tut tut! Tut tut!" said Robin.

"No, no, Mrs. Puss.   I saw you
catch a mouse yesterday, but you
shall not catch me."

Then the cat ran away to the
barn to look for another breakfast.

Just then a little girl came out to
hear Robin singing his song.   She
threw bread crumbs under the tree
and said,

> "Robin, Robin Redbreast,
> Singing on the bough,
> Come and get your breakfast,
> I will feed you now."

"Cheer-up, cheer-up! cheer-up,
cheer-up!" sang Robin.   This was
his way of saying, "Thank you!
Thank you!"

He flew down and had all the
breakfast he could eat.

THE GINGERBREAD BOY

Once there was a little old man, and a little old woman. They lived in a little old house.

The old woman made ginger-bread cakes.

One day she made a cake in the shape of a boy. She put it into the oven to bake.

When she opened the oven door, out jumped the Gingerbread Boy, and away he ran.

The little old man ran after him, but he could not catch him.

The Gingerbread Boy met a big man on the road. He said, "I

have run away from the little old woman. I can run away from you, too, so I can."

The big man ran after him, but he could not catch him.

The Gingerbread Boy met a cow. He said, "I have run away from a little old woman and a big man. I can run away from you, too. Yes, I can."

The cow ran after him, but she could not catch him.

Soon the Gingerbread Boy met a dog. He said, "I have run away from a little old woman, a big man, and a cow. I can run away from you, too. Yes, I can."

Then the dog ran after him. The dog ran very fast and caught

the Gingerbread Boy.   He began
to eat him.

The Gingerbread Boy said,
    "Oh, dear! my legs are gone!
    Oh, dear! my arms are gone!
    Oh, dear! my body is gone!
    Oh, dear! I am all gone!"
And he never spoke again.

———

East, west, home is best.

THE BEE

Buzz! Buzz!   This is the song of
    the bee;
His legs are of yellow, a jolly good
    fellow,
    And yet a great worker is he.

In days that are sunny
He's making his honey,
In days that are cloudy
He's making his wax.

Bees don't care
    about the snow;
I can tell you why
    that's so;
Once I caught
    a little bee,
Who was much too warm
    for me.

THE RATS AND THE EGG

One day two rats were eating an egg in a field.   They saw a fox coming toward them.

"The fox will eat our egg," said one rat.

"The fox will eat us, too, if we stay here," said the other rat.

"Now, what shall we do?" said both rats.

One rat lay down on his back. Then he let the other rat place the

egg between his feet, take hold of
his tail, and draw him to the barn
as fast as he could go.

The fox was afraid to come to
the barn, and the rats had a good
story to tell to their friends.

THE TOWN MUSICIANS

The donkey was old, and his master
was about to sell him.

"I shall not be sold," said the
donkey. "I will run away to town,
and join the band."

He met a dog upon the road.
"Come with me to town, and join
the band," said he. "You can beat
the drum."

"All right," said the dog.

They met an old cat by the way. "Come with us and help to make music," said they. "We have heard you sing."

"All right," said the cat.

Farther on, they met a rooster. "Come along and join our band," said they.

"All right," said the rooster.

At night they came to a large house in the woods. The donkey looked in through the high window. He saw robbers eating supper.

"I am so hungry," said the cat.

"Let us drive the robbers away," said the rooster.

"How shall we do it?" said the donkey.

"Let us frighten them," said the dog.

The donkey put his feet upon the sill of the window. The dog climbed upon his back. The cat climbed upon the dog's back. The rooster flew up and stood upon the cat's head. All looked in through the window.

Then they sang together with all their might. The donkey brayed, the dog barked, the cat mewed, and the rooster crowed. It was a dreadful noise.

It scared the robbers, who ran away as fast as they could.

The four friends sat down to

supper and ate what the robbers
had left.　Then they put out the
lights and waited.

An hour later one robber came
back.　He tried to light a candle
at the coals in the fireplace.　The
coals were the cat's eyes.　She
scratched him, the dog bit him, the
donkey kicked him, and the rooster
crowed at him.

He ran away at the top of his
speed.　He told the robbers that
he was never so scared in his life.
This made them all afraid, and they
never came back.

So the four friends made a home
for themselves in that house, and
never went to town.

THE LION AND THE MOUSE

One day a lion lay asleep in the woods.   A mouse ran over his nose.

The lion was about to eat him, but the mouse begged hard for his life.

"If you will let me go," he said, "I shall never forget you.   Some day I may be able to help you."

The lion smiled.   "Run away, little mouse," said he.   "I shall not hurt you."

Some days later hunters put a net in the lion's path. He fell into the net, and could not free himself.

The mouse heard him roar, and ran to him. "I will help you," said the mouse, and he began to gnaw the ropes.

It was hard work and slow, but at last the ropes fell apart, and the lion was free.

"How can I repay you for what you have done?" said the lion.

"You spared my life one day," said the mouse. "I am glad that I have been able to save yours."

———

Sing a song of winter;
Sing a song of spring;
In summer when the birds are here
No need a song to sing.

Once I saw a yellow bird on the
      grass.
I threw a bit of bread to him.
He looked glad and hopped near.
He took the bread in his beak.
Then he flew away to an apple tree.
He still had the bread in his beak.
He flew up to the top of the tree
      where there was a little nest.
Five little birds were in the nest.
He filled their mouths with the
      bread.
He flew away to another apple tree.
There he sang a loud, sweet song
      for me.

THE LITTLE MAN

Once there was a little boy.
He was only four years old.
He thought he was now very big.
One day he said,
    "I am not little any more.
I am almost as big as my father.
See, I can wear my father's hat!"
Then he put on his father's hat.
Then he took up his father's cane.
He went down the street for a walk.

The hat came down over his ears
and eyes.

The cane was higher than his head.

As he walked on, he felt very happy.

He was having a good time.

All the people laughed at him.

One man called out,

"Well, Hat, where is the boy?"

Another man called out,

"Well, Cane, where are you going
with the boy?"

THE DANDELION

"O dandelion, yellow as gold,
What do you do all day?"

"I just wait here in the long
green grass
Till the children come to play."

"O dandelion, yellow as gold,
What do you do all night?"

"I wait and wait till the cool dew
    falls
And my hair is long and white."

"What do you do when your hair
    grows white
And the children come to play?"

"They take me up in their dimpled
    hands
And blow my hair away."

HANS

Have you ever seen a bird like
this?   It is a stork.   There are
many of them in Holland where
little Hans lives.

One built its nest on the roof of
Hans' home.   It was a great pet,
and he fed it every day.

When cold weather comes, birds
fly away to where it is warm in
winter.   Hans knew his pet would
make its winter home in the warm
south.   He hoped some boy there
would be kind to it.

So he wrote a note and tied it to the bird's neck. The note said: "Please take care of my stork. Send it back to me next spring."

Winter came, and the stork flew south. When the warm days came again, Hans watched for his bird friend. At last he saw it coming, and it had a letter on its neck.

Hans fed his pet, and then read the letter. It said: "We cared for your stork, and now we send it back. The little children in our school want books. Can you help them?"

Hans and his father made up a box of books and sent them to the little people in the winter home of the stork.

A GIANT

Tom sat before the grate, reading. "I wish I could see a giant like those in this book," said he.

"I am one," said a voice in the grate. "Sometimes I am no bigger than the head of a match. Sometimes I am so big that it takes many men to fight me.

When men control me, I help them. I can roast beef, boil eggs, and bake bread. With my help men can make bricks and glass and knives.

When men let me go free, I often destroy houses and barns and crops, and even big forests.

Water is the only thing I am afraid of. Now, who am I?"

This little Indian boy lived in a wigwam with his grandmother, Nokomis. Have you ever seen a wigwam? Let me tell you where this wigwam was—

By the shining Big-Sea-Water,
Stood the wigwam of Nokomis.
Dark behind it rose the forest,
Bright before it beat the water,
Beat the clear and sunny water,
Beat the shining Big-Sea-Water.

Old Nokomis made him a little cradle. In it she put a bed of moss and rushes. When he cried, she used to say, "Hush! the bear will get thee!"

The boy learned the names of the birds. He learned how they built their nests in summer. He found where they hid themselves in winter. He learned how to talk with them. He called them his chickens.

He learned—

Where the squirrels hid their acorns,
How the reindeer ran so swiftly,
Why the rabbit was so timid.

He talked with them and called them his brothers. He learned their names and all their secrets.

When he grew older, he was given a bow and arrows. He went into the woods, but he did not shoot the birds, his chickens. He did not shoot the squirrels or the rabbits, his brothers.

He hid in the bushes till a red deer came. Then he shot an arrow, and the deer fell dead. He carried it home to his grandmother. She made a feast, and everybody came and praised the boy.

If you wish to be happy
      all the day,
Make others happy,—
      that's the way.

EVENING HYMN

Now the day is over,
  Night is drawing nigh,
Shadows of the evening
  Steal across the sky.

Now the darkness gathers,
  Stars begin to peep;
Birds, and beasts, and flowers
  Soon will be asleep.

Through the lonely darkness
  May the angels spread
Their white wings above me,
  Watching round my head.

When the morn awakens,
  Then may I arise,
Pure, and fresh, and sinless,
  In God's holy eyes.

These bunnies are looking through the
nursery window at their babies.

Ain't it fine when things are going
topsy turvey and askew,
To discover someone showing
good old fashioned faith in you.

THE ONTARIO READERS

FIRST BOOK

AUTHORIZED BY
THE MINISTER OF EDUCATION

PRICE 6 CENTS

TORONTO
T. EATON C°ᴸᴵᴹᴵᵀᴱᴰ
1-'30

FIRST READER

MORNING HYMN

FATHER, we thank Thee for the light,
And for the blessings of the night;
For rest and food, and loving care,
And all that makes the world so fair.

Help us to do the things we should,
To be to others kind and good;
In all we do, in work or play,
To grow more loving every day.

LITTLE THINGS

LITTLE drops of water,
   Little grains of sand,
Make the mighty ocean,
   And the pleasant land.

Little deeds of kindness,
   Little words of love,
Make our earth an Eden,
   Like the Heaven above.

THE SWING

How do you like to go up in a swing,
    Up in the air so blue?
Oh, I do think it the pleasantest thing
    Ever a child can do!

Up in the air and over the wall,
    Till I can see so wide,
Rivers and trees and cattle and all
    Over the countryside—

Till I look down on the garden green,
    Down on the roof so brown—
Up in the air I go flying again,
    Up in the air and down!

R. L. STEVENSON

THE HONEST INDIAN

AN old Indian once bought some things from a white man who kept a store.

When he got back to his wigwam and opened his bundle, he found some money in it.

"Good Luck!" thought the old Indian to himself. "I will keep this money. It will buy many things."

He went to bed, but he could not sleep. All night long he kept thinking about the money.

Over and over again he thought, "I will keep it." But something within him seemed to say: "No, no, you must not keep it; that would not be right."

Early the next morning he went back to the white man's store.

"Here is some money," said he; "I found it in my bundle."

"Why did you not keep it?" asked the store-keeper.

"There are two men inside me," replied the Indian. "One said: 'Keep it. You found it. The white man will never know.'

"The other said: 'Take it back!

Take it back! It is not yours! You have no right to keep it!'

"Then the first one said: 'Keep it! Keep it!'

"But the other kept saying: 'No! No! Take it back! Take it back!'

"The two men inside me talked all night. They would not let me sleep.

"I have brought the money back. Now the two men will stop talking. To-night I shall sleep."

A WISE old owl sat on an oak,
The more he saw, the less he spoke;
The less he spoke, the more he heard.
Why can't we all be like that bird?

THE LITTLE NUT

A LITTLE brown baby,
　　round and wee,
With kind winds
　　to rock him,
　　slept up in a tree;
And he grew
　　and he grew, till
　　—I'm sorry to say!

He fell right out of his cradle one day.

Down, down from the tree-top, a very bad
　　fall!
But this queer little fellow was not hurt
　　at all;
Now sound and sweet he lies down in the
　　grass,
And there you will find him whenever you
　　pass.

Do as you would be done by.

It is never too late to mend.

CRADLE SONG

Shut, little sleepy blue eyes;
Dear little head, be at rest;
Jesus, like you,
Was a baby once, too,
And slept on his own mother's
  breast.

Sleep, little baby of mine,
Soft on your pillow so white;
Jesus is here
To watch over you, dear,
And nothing can harm you to-night.

THE BOYS AND THE FROGS

Some boys, playing near a pond, saw a number of frogs in the water and began to pelt them with stones. One of the frogs, lifting his head above the water, cried out: "Boys, do stop: what is sport for you is not at all sport for us."

HOW DID HE DO IT

THERE was once a boy who had three goats.

All day long the three goats ran and played upon the hill.   At night the boy drove them home.

One night the frisky things jumped into a turnip field.   He could not get them out.

Then the boy sat down on the hillside and cried.

As he sat there a hare came along.

"Why do you cry?" asked the hare.

"I cry because I cannot get the goats out of the field," said the boy.

"I'll do it," said the hare.

So he tried, but the goats would not come.

Then the hare, too, sat down and cried.

Along came a fox. "Why do you cry?" asked the fox.

"I am crying because the boy cries," said the hare. "The boy is crying because he cannot get three goats out of the turnip field."

"I'll do it," said the fox.

So the fox tried to get them out of the field. But the goats would not come.

Then the fox, too, began to cry.

Soon after a wolf came along.

"Why do you cry?" asked the wolf.

"I am crying because the hare cries," said the fox. "The hare cries because the boy cries. The boy cries because he cannot get the three goats out of the turnip field."

"I'll do it," said the wolf.

He tried, but the goats would not leave the turnip field.

So he sat down with the others and began to cry, too.

After a little, a bee flew over the

hill and saw them all sitting there, crying.

"Why do you cry?" said the bee to the wolf.

"I am crying because the fox cries. The fox is crying because the hare cries. The hare cries because the boy cries. The boy cries because he cannot get the goats out of the turnip field."

"I'll do it," said the bee.

Then the big animals and the boy stopped crying a moment to laugh at the tiny bee.

But the bee flew away into the turnip field and alighted upon one of the goats, and said:

"Buz-z-z-z-z!"

And out ran the goats, every one!

EMILIE POULSSON

THREE LITTLE KITTENS

THREE little kittens lost their
    mittens,
And they began to cry,

    "O mother dear,
    We very much fear
    That we have lost our mittens."

  "Lost your mittens!
  You naughty kittens!
  Then you shall have no pie."

    "Mee-ow, mee-ow, mee-ow."

"No, you shall have no pie."

"Mee-ow, mee-ow, mee-ow."

The three little kittens found their
    mittens,
And they began to cry,

    "O mother dear,
    See here, see here!
    See! we have found our mittens."

"Put on your mittens,
You silly kittens,
And you may have some pie."

    "Purr-r, purr-r, purr-r,
    O let us have the pie.
    Purr-r, purr-r, purr-r."

The three little kittens put on their
    mittens,
And soon ate up the pie;

    "O mother dear,
    We greatly fear,
    That we have soiled our mittens."

"Soiled your mittens!
You naughty kittens!"

Then they began to sigh,
"Mee-ow, mee-ow, mee-ow."

The three little kittens washed
their mittens,
And hung them out to dry,

"O mother dear,
Do you not hear,
That we have washed our
mittens?"

"Washed your mittens!
O, you're good kittens.
But I smell a rat close by:
Hush! Hush!"

"Mee-ow, mee-ow.
We smell a rat close by,
Mee-ow, mee-ow, mee-ow."

THE CROWS AND THE WINDMILL

THERE was once a windmill that swung its arms round and round day after day. It did no harm to anybody.

But there was a flock of crows living near who did not like the busy mill. They said it wanted to kill some of them. What else could it mean by swinging its great arms the whole day long?

So all the crows met together one summer evening near the mill.

The younger crows all thought the mill a bad thing and wanted to pull it down at once.

Then an old crow said: "Does the windmill ever leave its place, and chase crows or hurt them?"

The crows had to own that it did not.

"How, then," asked the old crow, "is it likely to kill any of you?"

"Oh, it will do that if we go near it," they all said.

"And is that the only way that any of you will be hurt by it?"

"Yes, of course."

"Then," said the wise old crow, "I have only one thing to say: Keep out of harm's way."

WHAT DOES LITTLE BIRDIE SAY

What does little birdie say
In her nest at peep of day?
Let me fly, says little birdie,
Mother, let me fly away.

Birdie, rest a little longer,
Till the little wings are stronger.
So she rests a little longer,
Then she flies away.

What does little baby say,
In her bed at peep of day?
Baby says, like little birdie,
Let me rise and fly away.

Baby, sleep a little longer,
Till the little limbs are stronger.
If she sleeps a little longer,
Baby, too, shall fly away.

TENNYSON

A SECRET

I KNOW of a cradle, so wee and so blue,
Where a baby is sleeping this morning,—do
  you?

I think he is dreaming the dearest of
  things—
Of songs and of sunshine, of tiny brown
  wings.

I'll tell you a secret,—don't tell where you
  heard,—
The cradle's an egg,—and the baby's a bird!

Work while you work,
   Play while you play,
That is the way
   To be happy and gay.

THE WIND AND THE SUN

"I AM stronger than you are," said the cold, north wind.

"Indeed you are not," answered the bright, warm sun.

"Indeed, but I am."

"Indeed, but you are not."

"I will prove that I am stronger."

"You can't do that."

Just then a traveller was seen on the highway.

"I can get that traveller's coat off his back," said the cold, north wind.

" And I can make that traveller take his coat off in less time than you can," answered the bright, warm sun.

" Try it," roared the cold, north wind.

" You try it first," answered the bright, warm sun.

So the north wind blew a furious blast. The man was nearly blown down. The clasp of his coat was broken ; but he held it close about him and struggled on.

Again the north wind blew ; but the man only stood still, holding his coat closer until the blast was over.

"It is my turn now," said the sun. So he came out and poured his hot rays straight down upon the traveller.

"This is a strange climate," said the traveller; "first so cold, then so hot. I must take off this heavy coat, and here is a shady place beneath this tree where I will sit down and rest."

ÆSOP

———

Whichever way the wind doth blow,
Some heart is glad to have it so;
Then blow it east, or blow it west,
The wind that blows, that wind is best.

TWO LITTLE KITTENS

Two little kittens, one stormy night,
Began to quarrel, and then to fight.
One had a mouse, the other had none;
And that's the way the fight was begun.

"I will have the mouse," said the bigger
   cat.
"You will have the mouse! We'll see
   about that."
"I will have that mouse," said the older one.
"You shan't have that mouse,"
   said the little one.

I told you before 'twas a stormy night
When these two kittens began to fight.
The old woman took her sweeping broom,
And swept the two kittens out of the room.

The ground was covered with frost and snow,
And the two little kittens had nowhere to go;
So they laid them down on a mat
    at the door,
While the old woman finished sweeping
    the floor.

Then they crept in as quiet as mice,
All wet with snow and cold as ice;
For they thought 'twould be better,
    that stormy night,
To lie down and sleep than to quarrel and
    fight.

———

You never know, you cannot guess
What harm a little lie may do;
There's just one way that's safe and sure,
And that is just be always true.

KING SOLOMON AND THE BEES

Long, long ago there lived a King called Solomon. He was so wise that people came from all parts of the earth to visit him.

If there was a quarrel, he knew how to settle it; if there was anything lost, he knew where to find it; if there was any riddle, he could solve it.

One day a beautiful lady drove

up to his castle. She was very wealthy, for she was a Queen. She brought with her rich presents for the King. She talked with him for many hours, and she admired his great wisdom.

Before leaving she said she would test his power in a new way. She placed before the King two beautiful flowers. One was real, and the other was made of wax. But the two flowers looked exactly alike.

"Choose now, O King!" she said. "Tell me, after looking at them, which is the real flower, and which flower is made of wax."

For a long time the King looked at the flowers, but one seemed to be as real as the other. At last

he said: "We shall take the flowers
to the garden."

In the garden the bees were flying around, seeking for honey. They
came to the two flowers, but not
one of them entered the flower made
of wax.

"Now, O Queen!" he said, "I
can tell you which is the real
flower. My eyes cannot tell, but the
bees always go where the honey is."

THE SUNBEAM

See that little sunbeam
Darting through the room,
Lighting up the darkness,
Scattering the gloom.

Let me be a sunbeam
Everywhere I go,
Making glad and happy
Every one I know.

A KITTEN RHYME

SEE my kitty—little Dot.
Very pretty, is she not?
 Soft and silky
  Is her fur.
 If you stroke it,
  She will purr.
She's all white but one black spot.
That is why her name is Dot.
 Dot won't hurt you
  With her claws,
 Keeps them hidden
  In her paws.

Often when my Grandma knits,
Close beside her kitty sits,

>Watching, watching
>>Grandma's ball,
>Wishing she would
>>Let it fall.

When it does drop, oh! the fun!
You should see how Dot can run!

>Dot has never
>>Caught a rat.
>She's too little
>>Yet for that.

She is only good at play,
But she'll catch the rats some day.

EMILIE POULSSON

EARLY to bed,
And early to rise,
Makes a man healthy,
Wealthy, and wise.

OCTOBER'S PARTY

October gave a party;
The leaves by hundreds came,
The Chestnuts, Oaks, and Maples,
And leaves of every name.

The sunshine spread a carpet,
And everything was grand;
Miss Weather led the dancing,
Professor Wind the band.

The Chestnuts came in yellow,
The Oaks in crimson dressed,
The lovely Misses Maple
In scarlet looked their best.

All balanced to their partners
And gaily fluttered by;
The sight was like a rainbow
New fallen from the sky.

Then in the rustic hollow
At hide-and-seek they played;
The party closed at sundown,
And everybody stayed.

Professor Wind played louder;
They flew along the ground,
And then the party ended
In hands across, all round.

GEORGE COOPER

THE STAR

TWINKLE, twinkle, little star,
How I wonder what you are,
Up above the world so high,
Like a diamond in the sky.

When the glorious sun is set,
When the grass with dew is wet,
There you show your little light,
Twinkle, twinkle, all the night.

A GREAT NOISE

ONCE upon a time five rabbits lived near a lake in an old forest. One day they heard a great noise, and all ran away as fast as they could.

The foxes saw them running and called out: "Oh rabbits, why do you run so fast and look so scared?" The rabbits replied: "There was a great n o i s e." Then the foxes ran, too.

The bears saw the foxes running and asked: "Oh foxes, why do you run?" The foxes said: "There was a great noise." Then the bears ran, too.

The wolves saw the bears running and asked: "Oh bears, why do you run?" The bears answered: "There was a great noise." Then the wolves ran, too.

But one big, old wolf called out: "Why should we all run? We are strong and can fight. What was this noise?" The wolves said: "We do not know, but the bears said that there was a noise."

The wolf asked the bears and they replied: "We do not know, but the foxes said that there was a great noise." And the rabbits said: "We heard a great noise near our home and then we ran."

"Where is your home?" asked
the wolf.

"We live near the lake in the
forest," replied the rabbits.

"What was this noise like?"

"It was a crackling sound, loud
as thunder."

"Now," said the old wolf, "let
us all go to the lake and see what
this great noise was."

So the wolves and bears and
foxes and rabbits went together to
the lake, and what do you think
they found? Why, just a big tree
that had fallen into the water.

LADY MOON

Lady Moon, Lady Moon, where are you
　　　roving?
　　　"Over the sea."
Lady Moon, Lady Moon, whom are you
　　　loving?
　　　"All that love me."

Are you not tired with rolling, and never
　　　Resting to sleep?
Why look so pale and so sad, as for ever
　　　Wishing to weep?

"Ask me not this, little child, if you love me;
　　　You are too bold.
I must obey my dear Father above me,
　　　And do as I'm told."

Lady Moon, Lady Moon, where are you
　　　roving?
　　　"Over the sea."
Lady Moon, Lady Moon, whom are you
　　　loving?
　　　"All that love me."

Lord Houghton

————

Dare to be true; nothing can need
a lie.

THE HARE AND THE TORTOISE

ONCE upon a time a Hare overtook a Tortoise on a road that led to a large city.

"Good-morning, friend Tortoise," said the Hare.   "Where are you going to-day?"

"I am going to the river that flows through the city," said the Tortoise.

"That is a long way off," said the Hare, "and you are very slow. If you could run as fast as I can you would soon be there."

"Yet I might beat you in a race to the river," said the Tortoise.

"Done!" said the Hare. "Let us run a race and let the Fox be judge."

When they were ready, the Fox said : "One, two, three, go!" and away they went. The Hare was soon out of sight of the Tortoise. "That Tortoise will never catch me," he said, "I shall rest here for a few minutes." So he lay down in the grass and fell asleep.

The Tortoise kept on steadily till he came to the river.

When the Hare awoke from his nap, he could not see the Tortoise; so he said: "What a slow, old fellow he is!   I shall go back and look for him;" but after going back some distance he could not find him.   Then he said to himself: "I think I shall run on to the river, get a drink, and wait for the Tortoise."

When the Hare came racing down to the river, there sat the smiling Tortoise, waiting for him.

"Well! Well!" said the Fox, "I see that the race is not always won by the swift."

ÆSOP

A stitch in time saves nine.

WHAT I SHOULD DO

If I were a rose
On the garden wall,
I'd look so fair
And grow so tall;
I'd scatter perfume far and wide;
Of all the flowers I'd be the pride.
That's what I'd do
If I were you,
O little rose!

Fair little maid,
If I were you,
I should always try
To be good and true.
I'd be the merriest, sweetest child
On whom the sunshine ever smiled;
That's what I'd do
If I were you,
Dear little maid!

THE FOX AND THE CAT

ONE day a cat met a fox in the woods. Now the cat knew that the fox had seen a good deal of the world, and she thought him very clever and wise.

So she said: " Good-morning, Mr. Fox, how are you?"

The proud fox looked at her from head to foot and said: "How dare you ask me how I am! Do you think you are my equal? What can you do? How many tricks do you know?"

"I know just one trick," said the meek cat.

"And, pray, what is that?" asked the fox.

"Well," said the cat, "I can climb up a tree out of the way of dogs, and so save myself."

"Is that all?" said the fox. "Why, I know a hundred tricks. Come with me and I will show you how to baffle dogs."

Just then a pack of hounds came running through the woods. The cat sprang up into a tree and hid on a high branch. The fox ran for his life, but the hounds soon caught him.

"Ah, Mr. Fox," said the cat, "if you had known even one safe trick like mine, you would not have lost your life."

THE SNOW-FLAKES

SEE the pretty snow-flakes,
  Falling from the sky;
On the wall and house-tops,
  Soft and thick they lie.

On the window-ledges,
   On the branches bare,
See how fast they gather,
   Filling all the air.

Look into the garden,
   Where the grass was green;
Covered by the snow-flakes,
   Not a blade is seen.

Now the bare, black bushes
   All look soft and white;
Every twig snow-laden,
   What a pretty sight.

———

ONE step and then another,
   And the longest walk is ended;
One stitch and then another,
   And the largest rent is mended.

One flake upon another,
   And the deepest snow is laid;
One brick upon another,
   And the highest wall is made.

THE BELL OF ATRI

THE king of Atri built a tall
tower and hung a big bell in it.
A long rope hung from the bell to
the ground. "If any one does you
a wrong, ring this bell," said the
king, "then I shall know that some
one needs help."

Many people rang the bell—rich
people and poor people, big people
and little people. But at length

the rope was worn off till a man could hardly reach it. Some person, passing by, saw this and mended it with a long grape-vine.

Not far from the town lived a faithful old horse. He had worked for his master many years, and now he was too old to work any more. This unkind man would not feed him, but turned him out on the street to starve.

The poor horse wandered about until he saw the grape-vine. He was hungry and tried to eat it. This made the bell ring, and the king came to see who needed help. When he saw the starving horse, he sent for his master.

"This poor horse has served you well many years," said the king. "He is old now and cannot work. You must take him back to his stable, and feed and care for him for the rest of his life."

Then was the man ashamed, but he led home the horse and did as the king had ordered.

SNOW

THIS is the way the snow comes down,
Softly, softly falling;
So God giveth the snow like wool,
Fair and white and beautiful.
This is the way the snow comes down,
Softly, softly falling.

WHENE'ER a snow-flake leaves the sky,
It turns and turns to say: "Good-bye,
Good-bye, dear cloud, so cool and gray,"
Then lightly travels on its way.

THE BRIGHT SIDE

Nanny has a hopeful way,—
  Bright and sunny Nanny!
When I cracked the cup to-day,
  She said, in her hopeful way,
"It's only cracked; don't fret, I pray."
  Sunny, cheery Nanny!

Nanny has a hopeful way,
  So good, and sweet, and canny;
When I broke a cup to-day,
  She said, in her hopeful way,
"Well, 'twas cracked, I'm glad to say."
  Kindly, merry Nanny!

Nanny has a hopeful way,—
  Quite right, little Nanny;
Cups will crack and break alway,
  Fretting doesn't mend nor pay;
Do the best you can, I say,
  Busy, loving Nanny!

ALGERNON TASSIN

THE WOLF AND THE CAT

A Wolf ran out of a forest into a village, not because it wanted to go there, but because the hounds were hunting it.

It saw a cat sitting on a gate post and said, in its softest voice: "Thomas, my friend, tell me quickly who is the kindest man in the village, that I may hide in his barn from my foes. Do you hear the cry of the dogs who are in search of me?"

"Run quickly and ask Mr. Smith," said Thomas; "he is a kind man."

"True," said the wolf, "but I have killed one of his sheep."

"Well, then, try Mr. Brown."

"I fear he is vexed with me because I ate one of his goats."

"Suppose you try Mr. Jones."

"Mr. Jones! Why I carried off one of his calves last spring."

"So you have done harm to all these people. How can you expect help from those whom you have injured?"

"Oh, here are the hounds!" said the trembling wolf, and it raced away down the streets with the dogs close behind.

"Yes," said the cat, "what one sows he must reap."

THE WIND AND THE LEAVES

"Come, little leaves," said the wind one day;
"Come o'er the meadows with me, and play.
Put on your dresses of red and gold,—
Summer is gone, and the days grow cold."

Soon as the leaves heard the wind's loud call,
Down they came fluttering, one and all;
Over the brown fields they danced and flew,
Singing the soft little songs they knew.

Dancing and flying, the little leaves went;
Winter had called them, and they were
     content.
Soon fast asleep in their earthy beds,
The snow laid a blanket over their heads.

GEORGE COOPER

Whatever you do,
   Do with your might;
Things done by halves
   Are never done right.

THE DOG AND THE SHADOW

A DOG, crossing a stream with a piece of meat in his mouth, saw his own shadow in the clear water. He took the shadow he saw to be another dog.

"Aha!" said he, "I am in luck this morning. I have my breakfast in my mouth, and now I'll secure my dinner, too."

With that he snatched at the piece of meat which he saw in the shadow. But so far from getting the second piece, he dropped his own into the water. He was sadly put out to see that the other dog had dropped his, too.

He had to go home without his breakfast or dinner either, for his own piece had at once sunk to the bottom, away beyond his reach. The greedy dog had grasped at too much and had lost what he had.

ÆSOP

LOOK UP AND TRY

THREE little birdies up in a tree
  Come out of the nest to fly.
They all look up, and they all look down,
  And they chirp, "We are far too shy."

Three little birdies shake their heads,
　　When the old bird says, "Now try."
They all hop back, and they all sit down,
　　And they chirp, "We are far too high."
"Three little birdies, silly things,
　　Stay there, and you all will die!"
Off flies the old bird, and shakes her wings,
　　And says to them all, "Bye-bye."

Three little birdies hop from the nest
　　And chirp, "Now we all must try;
Out we must go to get nice fat worms,
　　For none of us wishes to die."
Three little birdies won't look down,
　　They all look up at the sky,
Off they all go, the three in a row,
　　And now they all can fly.

HOW THE PONY WAS SHOD

THERE was once a boy who owned a little gray pony. Every morning the boy would jump on his pony and ride away clippety, clippety, clap!

As he rode to town one day, he heard something fall with a clang on a stone in the road. He looked back and saw a horse-shoe. Down he leaped and looked at his pony's feet. Then he cried:

"What shall I do? What shall I do?
My little gray pony has lost a shoe!"

He made haste to go to the blacksmith and when he saw him he told him his trouble. But the blacksmith said:

"How can I shoe your pony's feet
Without some coal the iron to heat?"

The boy was downcast when he heard this. He left the pony in the smith's shop and went out to buy coal. He met a farmer coming to town and told him his trouble. The farmer said:

" I have bushels of corn and hay and
   wheat,
Something for you and your pony to eat;

But I have no coal the iron to heat,
That the blacksmith may shoe your
  pony's feet."

The boy turned away very sad.
Just then an old woman came down
the road, driving a flock of geese.
He told her all about his trouble,
and she laughed till her geese
began to cackle. Then she said:

" If you would know where the coal is
  found,
You must go to the miner who works in
  the ground."

He ran to the miner who had
lumps of black coal ready. He
took these in haste to the blacksmith who lit a great, red fire.
Then the smith beat out a fine,
new shoe, with a cling and a clang.

He put it on the pony's foot with a
tap and a rap, and away rode the
boy—clippety, clippety, clap!

MY LITTLE DOLL

I ONCE had a sweet little doll, dears,
  The prettiest doll in the world;
Her cheeks were so red and so white, dears,
  And her hair was so charmingly curled.
But I lost my poor little doll, dears,
  As I played in the heath one day,
And I cried for her more than a week, dears,
  But I never could find where she lay.

I found my poor little doll, dears,
  As I played in the heath one day;
Folks say she is terribly changed, dears,
  For her paint is all washed away,
And her arm trodden off by the cows, dears,
  And her hair not the least bit curled:
Yet for old sakes' sake she is still, dears,
  The prettiest doll in the world.

CHARLES KINGSLEY

LUCY OF THE LIGHTHOUSE

Lucy was a little girl who lived alone with her father in a lighthouse on a rocky island far out in the sea.

It was her father's work to take care of the large lamp in the lighthouse and at night to keep it always burning. The sailors who passed that way on the sea were thus able to steer their ships away from the rocks near by.

Lucy did not go to school because she lived so far away from the schools on the mainland; but her father taught her many things.

She went out on bright days and played in the sand. She was fond of the pretty shells and stones which she found there, and was as happy as any little girl can be.

Every night at sundown Lucy followed her father when he went up the many steps which led to the lamp in the lighthouse tower; and she watched him as he lighted the lamp and talked to him of the sailors who might be saved by it.

One day her father said to her: "They have brought us no food this week, and I must go to land in my boat to buy some. I will be back before dark."

Lucy watched his little boat till it was only a speck on the water; then it passed out of sight. She was a brave girl and had no fear of being alone.

Soon a black cloud came up, and then many clouds, and the sun was hidden. Rain began to fall in great drops, and Lucy took shelter in the lighthouse.

The storm was very wild, and the sea was very rough. From the window Lucy watched the giant waves. She knew her father could not come home in his little boat until the storm was over.

Soon night came on, and it was

very dark, and her father was not there to light the big lamp. Oh! if she could only light it, to show the way to her father and to the passing ships!

Although Lucy was a brave girl, she was lonely now and longed for her father. She climbed the stairs and tried to light the lamp as she had many times seen her father light it.

She was too short to reach the light. So she went down the stairs, and step by step carried up a chair and placed it under the lamp.

She mounted the chair and was glad to find that she could now reach high enough. She struck a match, for it was an oil lamp, and at once a great light shone out from the big lamp over the sea and toward the shore.

The storm soon ceased, and the great waves went down. Lucy was sure her father would soon come home.

By this time she was so tired that she could not keep awake, and she lay down on a rug near the lamp and fell sound asleep.

An hour or two afterwards her father returned, ran up the stairs as fast as he could, and saw the brave girl lying there asleep; and the lighthouse lamp was burning bright. Never was there a father more proud and happy.

ADAPTED

———————

Good to begin well;
Better to end well.

IF

IF I were a bird with a dear little nest,
  I should always be going for flights,
I'd fly to the North and the South and the
      West,
  And see all the wonderful sights.
I'd perch on the point of the very tall
      spires,
  And race with the insects and bees,
And there would be parties on telegraph
      wires,
  And school at the top of the trees.

If I were a fairy and lived in a flower,
  What fun, oh, what fun it would be!
I'm certain I never should sleep for an hour,
  And I'd always have honey for tea.
And never a stocking or shoe would I wear,
  Nor ever a hat on my head,
And no one would tell me to tidy my hair,
  And no one would send me to bed.

If I were a duchess in satin and pearls,
  I'd curtsey like this and like this;
I'd graciously smile at the lords and the earls,
  And give them my fingers to kiss.
And mother should dress all in silver and
    pink,
  And daddy in silver and green,
And off we should go in a coach, only think,
  To live with the King and the Queen!

ROSE FYLEMAN

To think kindly is good,
To speak kindly is better,
To act kindly is best.

THE SPIDER AND THE FLY

"WILL you walk into my parlour?"
   Said the Spider to the Fly;
"'Tis the prettiest little parlour
   That ever you did spy.

" The way into my parlour
   Is up a winding stair,
And I have many curious things
   To show when you are there."

"Oh no, no," said the little Fly,
   "To ask me is in vain;
For who goes up your winding stair
   Can ne'er come down again."

" I'm sure you must be weary, dear,
   With soaring up so high;
Will you rest upon my little bed?"
   Said the Spider to the Fly.

"There are pretty curtains drawn around;
   The sheets are fine and thin,
And if you like to rest awhile,
   I'll snugly tuck you in."

"Oh no, no," said the little Fly,
  "For I've often heard it said,
They never, never wake again,
  Who sleep upon your bed."

"Sweet creature!" said the Spider,
  "You're witty and you're wise;
How handsome are your gauzy wings!
  How brilliant are your eyes!

"I have a little looking-glass
  Upon my parlour shelf;
If you'll step in one moment, dear,
  You shall behold yourself."

"I thank you, gentle sir," she said,
  "For what you're pleased to say,
And, bidding you good-morning now,
  I'll call another day."

The Spider turned round and
went into his den. He knew the
silly little Fly would soon come
back to hear him say flattering

words about her, and she did.
Then he caught her and

—dragged her up his winding stair,
   Into his dismal den,
Within his little parlour—
   But she ne'er came out again.

MARY HOWITT
(Adapted)

THE HONEST WOODMAN

A WOODMAN, who was cutting wood on the banks of a river, let his axe fall into the water. He at once began to pray to the gods to find it for him.

Mercury appeared and asked him what was the matter.

"I have lost my axe," said he.

When Mercury heard this, he dived into the water and brought up a golden axe.

"Is this your axe?" said Mercury.

"It is not," said the man.

Next time Mercury brought up a silver one. "Is this one yours?" "No," said the woodman again.

The third time Mercury brought up an iron one, which the man said was his, as soon as he saw it.

"It is yours," said Mercury, "and for your honesty I shall give you the other two, also."

———

Do not judge a thing by its size. Sometimes little things are better than big things.

THE RAINBOW

Two little clouds one summer's day
   Went flying through the sky;
They went so fast they bumped their
     heads,
   And both began to cry.

Old Father Sun looked out, and said:
   "Oh! never mind, my dears,
I'll send my little fairy folk
   To dry your falling tears."

One fairy came in violet,
   And one in indigo;
In blue, green, yellow, orange, red—
   They made a pretty row.

They wiped the cloud-tears all away,
   And then, from out the sky,
Upon a line the sunbeams made,
   They hung their gowns to dry.

LIZZIE HADLEY

A soft answer turneth away
wrath, but grievous words stir up
anger.

PROVERBS, XV, 1

THE FIELD MOUSE AND THE TOWN MOUSE

A YOUNG Field Mouse had a friend who lived in a house in the town. Now the Town Mouse was asked by  the Field Mouse to dine with him. So one morning he went out to the country to visit his friend. At noon they sat down to a meal of dry corn and wheat, It was the best food that the Field Mouse could get.

"Do you know, my friend," said the Town Mouse, "that you live a mere ant's life out here? Are you content to live on corn and wheat for the rest of your life? Why, at home I have all kinds of good things. Come with me to town and enjoy them."

"I shall be very glad to go with you," said the Field Mouse, so the two set off for town. It was night when they got to the fine house in which the Town Mouse lived. They soon sat down to a meal of cheese and cream and bread and honey.

"You are right," said the Field Mouse, "it is much better to live here than in the country."

Just then a big cat came into the pantry. "Run," said the Town Mouse, and they hid in a hole. When the cat left the room, they came out to finish their meal; but before they could get to the table a big dog jumped in. "Run for your life," said the Town Mouse, and they hid again in a hole.

Then the Field Mouse said: "Do as you like, my friend, eat all you want, have your fill of good things, but you must be in fear of your life every day. I will go back to the country where I have simple food, but where, at least, I can eat it in peace."

So he said good-bye to his town friend and ran back to the country as fast as he could.

CHERRIES

UNDER the tree the farmer said,
Smiling and shaking his wise old head:
"Cherries are ripe! but then, you know,
There's the grass to be cut and the corn to
　　hoe;
We can gather the cherries any day,
But when the sun shines we must make our
　　hay;
To-night, when the work has all been done,
We'll muster the boys, for fruit and fun."

Up on the tree a robin said,
Perking and shaking his saucy head:

"Cherries are ripe! and so to-day
We'll gather them while you make the hay;
For we are the boys with no corn to hoe,
No cows to milk, and no grass to mow."
At night the farmer said: "Here's a trick!
These roguish robins have had their pick."

F. E. WEATHERLEY

THE FOUR PEACHES

ONCE upon a time four brothers lived together. They were rich and happy. But one day a great storm swept over the land, and their barns and houses were blown down, and their cattle killed.

Now, in that land, there lived a very wise man, and the brothers went to him and told him of their hard luck. He had pity on them and gave each of them a wonderful peach.

"Put your peach on your head," he said to each, "and go your way. Where the peach falls, there dig, and what your spade uncovers, that take and be glad." So they went out together.

When they had gone a mile, one peach fell to the ground. Its owner dug and found Copper. "Good!" said he to his brothers; "stay with me and share in my luck." But they thought they could do better, and went on.

In a short time the second man's peach fell, and he dug and found Silver. "Better still!" said he; "stay with me, brothers, and share my fortune." But they thought they might do better, and went on.

Soon the third man's peach fell,

and he dug and found Gold. "Best of all!" cried he. "Brother, stay here, take half my fortune, and be glad with me." But the fourth man thought he might find Diamonds, and went on.

Well, after a long walk, his peach fell, and, after much digging, he found Iron. He was sad. He did not know which was of greater use, Diamonds or Iron. Do you?

THERE are no fairy folks that ride
About the world at night,
And give you rings and other things,
To pay for doing right;
But, if you do to others what
You'd have them do to you,
You'll be as blest as if the best
Of story-books were true.

ALICE CARY

GRAY AND WHITE

THERE was once a rab-
   bit with silver fur:
Her little gray neigh-
   bours looked up to
   her,
Till she thought with
   pride in the moon-lit
   wood,
" The reason I'm white
   is because I'm good."

" Oh what shall I do?" cried a tiny mole;
" A fairy has tumbled into a hole:
It's full of water and crawling things,
And she can't get out, for she's hurt her
   wings.

" I did my best to catch hold of her hair,
But my arms are so short, and she's still in
   there,
Oh! darling white rabbit, your arms are long,
You say you are good, and I know you are
   strong."

" Don't tell me about it," the rabbit said,—
She shut up her eyes, and her ears grew
    red ;—
" There's lots of mud, and it's sure to stick,
Because my hair is so long and thick."

" Oh dear! oh dear!" sobbed the poor little
    mole,
" Who will help the fairy out of the hole? "
A common gray rabbit popped up from the
    gorse,
" I'm not very strong, but I'll try, of course."

His little tail bobbed as he waded in,
The muddy water came up to his chin,
But he caught the fairy tight by the hand
And sent her off safe into Fairy-land.

But she kissed him first on his muddy nose,
She kissed his face, and his little wet toes,
And when the day dawned, in the early light
That little gray rabbit was shining white.

Honour thy father and thy mother, that thy
days may be long in the land.

THE LITTLE GRAY KITTEN

ONCE upon a time there was a little gray kitten who had wandered far away from home.

At first she liked all the strange sights she saw, but by and by she began to feel very homesick, and wished she were once more cuddled up with her brothers and sisters.

Now the only word that this

little gray kitten knew was "Mew!"
So when she was lonely, she would
say "Mew!" When she was hungry, she would say "Mew!" When
she was cold or tired, glad or sad,
it was always "Mew!"

At home they knew what she
meant when she said "Mew!" but
out in the wide, wide world nobody
seemed to know.

Wandering along the street, she
came upon a little squirming earthworm. "Mew?" said she, meaning
"Where is my home?"

The earthworm, however, did not
notice the little gray kitten but
crawled away across the street.

Next, the little gray kitten met
a butterfly on the top of a dandelion. "Mew?" said the little gray

kitten, meaning "Can you tell me where my home is?"

But the butterfly did not say anything and flew away.

The little gray kitten walked on, and then she spied a robin on a stone wall near by. "Mew?" said the little gray kitten, meaning "Where is my home?"

But the robin, cocking his head to one side, answered, "Chirp, chirp!" Then spreading his wings, he flew away.

The little gray kitten felt very sad indeed, but running along, she came up to a big black dog. "Mew, mew?" said the little gray kitten, meaning "Oh, can you tell me where my home is?"

But the big black dog shook his

tail and barked, "Bow-wow, bow-wow, bow-wow!" so loudly that the little gray kitten ran away from him as fast as she could go.

The little gray kitten was very tired, but she still ran on and soon met a big red cow. "Mew, mew?" said the little gray kitten, meaning "Where is my home?"

The big red cow, however, hardly looking at the little kitten, stretched out her big head and shouted, "Moo, moo-oo!" This frightened the little gray kitten so much that she jumped over a fence and right into the middle of a flower-bed.

There she caught sight of a little girl running up to her with such a sweet smile on her face that the little gray kitten ran to her and said once more, "Mew, mew?" meaning "Do you know where my home is?"

"Oh, you dear fluffy gray ball," said the smiling little girl, catching the kitten up in her arms. "I'm going to take you right home to live with me."

The little girl was the only one who had understood, and the little gray kitten purred softly. She was happy, for she had found a home at last.

MARY LAWRENCE TURNBULL

———

Kind hearts are the gardens,
Kind thoughts are the roots,
Kind words are the flowers,
Kind deeds are the fruits.

THREE BUGS

Three little bugs in a basket,
  And hardly room for two!
And one was yellow, and one was black,
  And one like me or you.
The space was small, no doubt, for all;
  But what should three bugs do?

Three little bugs in a basket,
  And hardly crumbs for two;
And all were selfish in their hearts,
  The same as I or you;
So the strong ones said: "We will eat
    this bread,
  And that is what we'll do!"

Three little bugs in a basket,
　　And the beds but two would hold;
So they all three fell to quarrelling,—
　　The white and the black and gold;
And two of the bugs got under the rugs,
　　And one was out in the cold!

So he that was left in the basket,
　　Without a crumb to chew,
Or a thread to wrap himself about,
　　When the wind across him blew,
Pulled one of the rugs from one of the
　　　bugs,
　　And so the quarrel grew!

And so there was war in the basket,
　　Ah, pity 'tis, 'tis true!
But he that was frozen and starved at
　　　last
　　A strength from his weakness drew,
And pulled the rugs from both of the
　　　bugs,
　　And killed and ate them, too!

Now when bugs live in a basket,
    Though more than it well can hold,
It seems to me they had better agree,—
    The white and the black and the gold,
And share what comes of the beds and
        the crumbs,
    And leave no bug in the cold.

                                    ALICE CARY

THE FROG PRINCE

IN the old far-off days there lived a young princess so beautiful that even the sun, which sees a great many things, had never seen her equal. When she was dull, she played with a golden ball, tossing it and catching it.

One day, as she sat playing near a deep well her ball rolled into it. At this she began to cry and sob and was very unhappy.

Just then a frog put his head out of the water and said: "What ails you?" The princess told him.

"What will you give me if I bring your ball up to you?" said the frog.

"Anything you may ask," replied the princess.

"If you will love me, and let me sit by you at your own table, and eat off your little golden plate, and be your friend—if you promise this —I will dive for your ball," said he.

"Oh, yes," said she, "I promise all you ask, only bring back my ball."

No sooner had the frog brought back the ball than the princess picked it up and ran away with it to the palace, leaving the frog behind.

Next day, as the king and his family sat at dinner, a knock was heard at the door, and a voice said:

"Princess, youngest princess!
Open the door for me!
Have you forgotten what befell
Yesterday by the side of the well?"

The princess told her father who it was and what she had promised. Then said the king: "You must do what you said you would. Go and let him in." She did so and the frog hopped along to the table.

"Lift me up," said the frog, "and put me on the table." But she would not until her father bade her do it. "Now, push your little golden plate nearer to me that we may eat together."

When she refused, because she was afraid of the frog, her father said: "You ought not to feel so toward one who helped you when you were in trouble. What you have promised you must do."

So she moved her little golden plate nearer to him, and they ate together. When she had done her dinner, she began to feel less afraid of the frog, and in the afternoon she played with him for some time.

Next morning the strangest thing had happened. The frog was nowhere to be seen, but at the top of the stairs she found a charming young prince waiting for her. He told her how he had been changed into a frog by a wicked fairy and shut up in the well, and that no one but the most beautiful princess who would make a friend of him could change him back again.

THE QUEER LITTLE HOUSE

There's a queer little house, and it stands
   in the sun.
When the good mother calls, the children
   all run.
While under her roof they are cosy and
   warm,
Though the cold wind may whistle and
   bluster and storm.

In the daytime this queer little house moves
away,

And the children run after it, happy and
gay;

But it comes back at night, and the children
are fed

And tucked up to sleep in a soft feather-bed.

This queer little house has no windows nor
doors—

The roof has no shingles, the rooms have no
floors—

No fireplaces, chimneys, nor stoves can you
see,

Yet the children are cosy and warm as can
be.

The story of this funny house is all true;

I have seen it myself, and I think you have,
too.

You can see it to-day, if you watch the old
hen,

When her downy wings cover her chickens
again.

LITTLE THINGS

Two men were at work one day in a shipyard. They were hewing a piece of timber to put into a ship. It was a small piece and not worth much. As they cut off the chips, they found a worm, a little worm about half an inch long, in the wood.

"This wood is wormy," said one; "shall we put it in?"

"I don't know: yes, I think it may go in: it will never be seen, of course."

"Yes; but there may be other worms in it, and these may increase and injure the ship."

"No, I think not. To be sure the wood is not worth much; but

I do not wish to lose it. Come, never mind the worm, we have seen but one; put it in."

So the wormy piece of wood was put in. The ship was made, and she looked very noble, indeed. She went to sea, and for a number of years did well. But it was found, on a distant voyage, that she grew weak and rotten. Her timbers were found to be much eaten by worms. The captain tried to get her home, but she sprang a leak. She filled with water and soon after sank, with most of the crew and all the goods on board.

You see that a fine ship and many lives may be lost through a

little worm! And how much evil
may a man do when he does a
small wrong, as he did who put
the wormy timber into the ship!

ALICE

DANCING on the hilltops,
   Singing in the valleys,
Laughing with the echoes,
   Merry little Alice.

Playing games with lambkins
   In the flowering valleys,
Gathering pretty posies,
   Helpful little Alice.

If her father's cottage
   Turned into a palace,
And he owned the hilltops
   And the flowering valleys,
She'd be none the happier,
   Happy little Alice.

CHRISTINA ROSSETTI

THE FOX AND THE HEN

A HUNGRY fox was one day looking for a poultry-yard. As he was passing a farmhouse, he saw a hen and some chickens which had gone up into a tree for the night. He drew near and invited them to come down and rejoice with him on account of the fact that peace had been made among the animals.

The hen said she was glad of it, but that she did not intend to come down before the next morning. "But," said she, "I see two dogs coming; I have no doubt they will be glad to celebrate with you the making of peace."

Just then the fox remembered that he had business elsewhere, and, bidding the hen good-bye, began to run.

"Why do you run?" said the hen. "If the animals have made a peace, the dogs will not hurt you. I know them; they are good, honest dogs, and would not harm any one."

"Ah," said the fox, "I fear they have not yet heard the news."

SPRING WAKING

SNOWDROP lay in the sweet,
dark ground,
"Come out," said the Sun,
"come out!"
But she lay quite still
and she heard no
sound;
"Asleep," said the Sun,
"no doubt!"

The Snowdrop heard, for she raised her head,
"Look spry," said the Sun, "look spry!"
"It's warm," said the Snowdrop, "here in
bed."
"Oh, fie!" said the Sun, "oh, fie!"

"You call too soon, Mr. Sun, you do!"
"No, no," said the Sun, "oh, no!"
"There's something above and I can't see
through."
"It's snow," said the Sun, "just snow."

"But I say, Mr. Sun, are the Robins here?"
  "Maybe," said the Sun, "maybe."
"There wasn't a bird when you called last
    year."
  "Come out," said the Sun, "and see!"

The Snowdrop sighed, for she liked her nap,
  And there wasn't a bird in sight,
But she popped out of bed in her white
    night-cap;
  "That's right," said the Sun, "that's
    right!"

And, soon as that small night-cap was seen,
  A Robin began to sing,
The air grew warm, and the grass turned
    green.
"'Tis spring!" laughed the Sun, "'tis
    spring!"

ISABEL ECCLESTONE MACKAY

It was only a sunny smile,
And little it cost in the giving,
    But it scattered the night,
    Like the morning light,
And made the day worth living.

THE PIED PIPER

MANY years ago the little town of Hamelin was overrun with rats— big, fierce rats.

They fought the dogs and killed the cats
And bit the babies in the cradles
And ate the cheeses out of the vats
And made nests inside men's Sunday hats.

Every one tried to think of some plan by which the rats could be driven out. When many plans had failed, the people came to the town-hall to tell the Mayor that he must do something.

The Mayor said he would give anything he had to the man who would rid the town of these rats. As he was speaking, a knock was heard at the door.

" Bless us ! " cried the Mayor, " What's
    that ?
Anything like the sound of a rat
Makes my heart go pitapat ! "

The door opened and in came a man whom no one there had ever seen before. He wore a long coat, half of yellow and half of red, and carried a pipe or flute.

" Who are you ? " said the Mayor.

"I am called the Pied Piper," said the stranger, "and I can rid your town of rats."

"I will give you a thousand pieces of gold if you will do so," said the Mayor.

The Piper went into the street and began to play a tune. In a few minutes

—out of the houses the rats came tumbling—

Great rats, small rats, lean rats, brawny rats,

Brown rats, black rats, gray rats, tawny rats,

and followed the Piper, dancing to his music. He led them to the river and into it they went, and all were drowned.

When the Piper came back for his fee, the Mayor gave him only fifty pieces.

"Give me the money you promised or you will be sorry," said the Piper.

"The rats are all dead," said the Mayor.

Then the Piper went out into the street and began to play a sweeter tune than before.

Out came the children running:
All the little boys and girls,
With rosy cheeks and flaxen curls,
And sparkling eyes and teeth like pearls.

The Piper went down the street and out into the field. The children ran after him, skipping and singing. When they came to the mountain, a door opened and in they all marched, and then the door closed for ever.

The Mayor sent men north and south, east and west, to find the Piper. " Tell him," said he, "that I will give him all the money in Hamelin if he will bring our children back." But no one has ever seen Piper or children since.

This is not a true story. It is just a fairy tale to teach us if we make a promise we must not break it. The mayor would not pay the piper the money he promised, so the piper punished him by taking all the children into the mountain and back to his country to live with him.

THE BABY SWALLOW

On a belfry turret's
　　Weather-beaten breast,
Lo! a Baby Swallow
　　Perches on his nest.

"Courage!" says the
　　　Mother,
　"Spread out either wing,
Spread it quite out in the
　　　wind,
　And then forward spring."

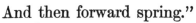

　　Baby Swallow pauses;
　　　"O how deep!" he cries,—
　"And my wings are far too small!—"
　　　Mother-Bird replies:

　"When, from off our house-top,
　　　First myself I threw,
　The good God—He carried me,
　　　Quite as small as you."

Baby Swallow lightly
  Spreads out both his wings,
Spreads them quite out in the wind,
  And then forward springs.

O surprise!—he's flying!
  Nothing more he fears;
Round about the church he goes,
  And how well he steers!

Mother-Bird beside him,
  Singing full and strong,
To the God who carried him,
  All her swallow-song.

From the French of RAMBERT

A busy spider made a web
  Of thread so very fine,
Your little fingers scarce could feel
  The tiny slender line.
Round-about, and round-about,
  And round-about it spun,
Straight across and back again,
  Until the web was done.

Itsy Bitsy spider climbed up a birthday cake.
But Itsy Bitsy spider made a big mistake.
He climbed up a candle before the cake was cut.
And Itsy Bitsy spider burnt his little butt.

THE LITTLE ACORN

IT was a little acorn that hung on the bough of a tree.

It had a tender green cup and a beautifully carved saucer to hold it.

The mother oak fed it with sweet sap every day, the birds sang good-night songs above it, and the wind rocked it gently to and fro. The oak leaves made a soft, green shade above it, so that the sun might not shine too warmly on its green cover. It was as happy as an acorn could be.

There were many other acorns on the tree, and the mother tree, through her wind voices, whispered loving words to all her babies.

The summer days were so bright and pleasant that the acorn never thought of anything but sunshine and a shower now and then to wash away the dust.

But summer ended, and the autumn days came. The green cup of the acorn turned to a brown cup, and it was well that it grew stiffer and harder, for the cold winds began to blow.

The leaves turned from green to golden brown, and some of them were whisked away by the rough wind. The little acorn began to feel uneasy.

"Isn't it always summer?" it asked.

"Oh, no," whispered the mother

oak. "The cold days come, and the leaves must fall, and the acorns, too. I must soon lose my babies."

"Oh, but I could never leave this kind bough," said the frightened acorn. "I should be lost and forgotten if I were to fall."

So it tried to cling all the closer to its bough; but at last it was alone there. The leaves were blown away, and some of them had made a blanket for the brown acorns lying on the ground.

One night the tree whispered a message to the lonely acorn. "This tree is your home only for a time. This is not your real life. Your brown shell is only the cover for a living plant, which can never be set free until the hard shell drops away.

This will happen after you are buried in the ground and the spring calls you.

"So, let go, little acorn, and fall to the ground, and some day you will wake to a new and glorious life."

The acorn listened and believed, for was not the tree its mother? It bade her good-bye, and, loosening its hold, dropped to the ground.

Then, indeed, it seemed as if the acorn were lost. That night a high wind blew and covered it deep under a heap of oak leaves.

The next day a cold rain washed the leaves closer together, and trickling water from the hillside covered them with earth. The acorn was buried.

"But I shall wake again," it said; and it fell asleep. The winter was cold; but the frost fairies wove a soft, white, snow blanket to cover the acorn and to keep it warm.

If you had walked through the woods that winter, you would have said that the acorn was gone. But spring came and called to all the sleeping things underground to waken and come forth.

The acorn heard and tried to move, but the brown shell held it fast. Some raindrops trickled through the ground to moisten the shell; and one day the pushing life within it set it free.

The brown shell was of no more use and was lost in the ground, but the young plant lived. It heard

voices of birds calling it upwards. It
must grow. "A new and glorious
life!" the mother oak had said.

"I must rise," said the young
plant; and up it came, up into
the world of sunshine and beauty.
It looked around. It saw the green
moss in the woods; it heard the
singing brook.

"Now I know that I shall live and grow," said the little plant.

"Yes," rustled the mother oak, "you are now a young oak tree. This is your real life."

And the little oak tree was glad and stretched higher and higher toward the sun.

LUCY WHEELOCK

THE DANDELION

THERE was a pretty dandelion,
With lovely, fluffy hair,
That glistened in the sunshine
And in the summer air.

But oh! this pretty dandelion
Soon grew quite old and gray;
And, sad to tell, her charming hair
Blew many miles away.

THE SEED AND THE STONE

A TINY seed lay asleep in the ground. The cold winter had gone, and spring had come.

The soft rain fell, and the sun shone bright. The earth was warm and damp.

The little seed woke up. "Dear me," it said, "what a nice sleep I have had! I must begin to grow now."

A little stone lay at its side. "Grow?" said the stone; "what do you mean? *I* never grow."

"That is a pity," said the seed. "I was put here to sleep and then to grow. Just wait, and you will see."

First, the seed began to swell.

Its coat was soon too small for it and split right down the back.

"Poor thing, you will break up and die," said the stone. "No, no!" was the reply. "I am only growing."

Then the seed pushed a tiny white foot down into the soft earth. "There is my foot," it said. "That will hold me firm while I grow."

Next, it pushed its head up above the ground. Its old coat fell off, and two tiny, green leaves came out.

"Now I can see the sun, and I breathe the sweet air, and I feel the cool rain," said the seed. "I am growing every day; I shall soon be a big plant."

"Dear me, this is very odd," said the stone. "I never knew that things could grow like this."

"Good-bye, my friend," said the seed, which was now a little plant. "I will grow ever so high yet. By-and-by I shall throw down seeds of my own beside you. Tell them to go to sleep till the spring comes, and then they too will grow."

THE LAUGHING BROOK

"Why do you laugh, little brook, little brook,
    And why so dimpled and gay?
What did you hear as you came through the wood,
    And what did you see on the way?"

"Such fun as I've had!   I saw in the wood
    The violets opening their eyes,
The little ferns straightening out their curls,
    And Jack-in-the-Pulpit rise.

The sunbeams, in passing, threw me a kiss;
    The breezes whispered to me;
And the tiny pebbles tickled me so
    I couldn't help laughing, you see."

ELIZABETH SCANTLEBURY

THE STORY OF MOSES

ONCE there lived in Egypt a king named Pharaoh, who made a wicked law. By this law all Hebrew boys, as soon as they were born, had to be cast into the river.

One poor mother, to save her little son, hid him for three months. But when she could hide him no longer, she put him in a small basket, made of bulrushes covered with pitch. Then she placed the basket among the rushes by the side of the river.

And the daughter of the king came down to the river to bathe. When she saw the basket, she sent her maid to fetch it. She found inside the basket a little babe crying. She took pity on the child and said:

"This is one of the Hebrew children."
So she sent for a nurse, and the little
child's mother was brought to her.

And the king's daughter said to
the Hebrew woman: "Take this
child away and nurse it for me, and
I will give thee thy wages." So the
child's mother took him and nursed
him.

When the child grew up, he was
taken to the king's daughter, and he
became her son. She called him
Moses, because, as she said: "I drew
him out of the water."

When Moses was grown up, and
a new king ruled over Egypt, God
chose Moses to lead the Hebrews
out of Egypt, for they were very
cruelly treated there. But the king
did not want to let them go. So God

gave Moses and Aaron, his brother, the power to do many wonders in the land of Egypt and to smite the people of Egypt with many plagues.

At last, after many days, the king of Egypt let the Hebrew people go. But as soon as they had gone, the king collected a great army and followed them, in order to destroy them.

And the Hebrews were much afraid when they saw the king's army behind them. But Moses said unto his people: "Fear not, stand still; the Lord shall fight for you."

Then God caused the waters of the Red Sea, which was in front of them, to divide; and they went on dry ground through the midst of the sea; and "the waters were a wall unto them on their right hand and on their left."

When the people of Egypt also tried to cross, Moses stretched forth his hand over the sea, and the waters covered them and drowned them all.

Thus the Lord that day saved the "Children of Israel", as the Hebrews were called, and destroyed the people of Egypt.

SPRING

THE alder by the river
    Shakes out her powdery curls;
The willow buds in silver
    For little boys and girls.

The little birds fly over,
    And oh, how sweet they sing!
To tell the happy children
    That once again 'tis Spring.

The gay green grass comes creeping
   So soft beneath their feet.
The frogs begin to ripple
   A music clear and sweet.

And buttercups are coming,
   And scarlet columbine,
And in the sunny meadows
   The dandelions shine.

And just as many daisies
   As their soft hands can hold,
The little ones may gather,
   All fair in white and gold.

Here blows the warm red clover,
   There peeps the violet blue;
O happy little children!
   God made them all for you.

CELIA THAXTER

Back of the bread is the snowy flour;
Back of the flour is the mill;
Back of the mill are the wheat and the
   shower,
The sun and the Father's will.

THE REASON WHY

"WHEN I was at the party,"
　　Said Betty (aged just four),
"A little girl fell off her chair,
　　Right down upon the floor;
And all the other little girls
　　Began to laugh, but me—
I didn't laugh a little bit,"
　　Said Betty, grave and wee.

"Why not?" her mother asked her,
　　Full of delight to find
That Betty—bless her little heart!—
　　Had been so sweetly kind.
"Why didn't *you* laugh, darling?
　　Or don't you like to tell?"
"I didn't laugh," said Betty,
　　"'Cause I'm the girl that fell!"

　　　　　　　　　　　M. E. BRADLEY

Hearts, like doors, will ope with ease
To very, very little keys;
And don't forget that two are these:
"I thank you, sir," and "If you please."

BIRD THOUGHTS

I LIVED first in a little house,
   And lived there very well;
I thought the world was small and round
   And made of pale blue shell.

I lived next in a little nest,
   Nor needed any other;
I thought the world was made of straw,
   And brooded by my mother.

One day I fluttered from the nest,
   To see what I could find.
I said: "The world is made of leaves—
   I have been very blind."

At length I flew beyond the tree,
   Quite fit for grown-up labours.
I don't know *how* the world is made,
   And neither do my neighbours.

If a task is once begun,
Never leave it till it's done.

EVENING HYMN

THE hours of day are over,
   The evening calls us home;
Once more to Thee, O Father,
   With thankful hearts we come.

For life and health, and shelter
   From harm throughout the day,
The kindness of our teachers,
   The gladness of our play;

For all the dear affection
   Of parents, brothers, friends,
To Him our thanks we render
   Who these and all things sends.

Lord, gather all Thy children
   To meet in Heaven at last,
When earthly tasks are ended,
   And earthly days are past.

THE ONTARIO READERS

SECOND BOOK

**AUTHORIZED BY
THE MINISTER OF EDUCATION**

PRICE 9 CENTS

TORONTO

T. EATON C℁ᴸᴵᴹᴵᵀᴱᴰ

2-'30

Following are selected parts of the
second reader as well as a few additions.

THE LAND OF STORY-BOOKS

AT evening when the lamp is lit,
Around the fire my parents sit ;
They sit at home and talk and sing,
And do not play at anything.

Now, with my little gun, I crawl
All in the dark along the wall,
And follow round the forest track
Away behind the sofa back.

There, in the night, where none can spy,
All in my hunter's camp I lie,
And play at books that I have read
Till it is time to go to bed.

These are the hills, these are the woods,
These are my starry solitudes;
And there the river by whose brink
The roaring lions come to drink.

I see the others far away,
As if in fire-lit camp they lay,
And I like to an Indian scout,
Around their party prowled about.

So, when my nurse comes in for me,
Home I return across the sea,
And go to bed with backward looks
At my dear land of Story-books.

R.L. STEVENSON

They that go down to the sea in ships,
  that do business in great waters;
These see the works of the Lord,
  and His wonders in the deep.

PSALM CVII, 23, 24

SEPTEMBER

THE goldenrod is yellow;
  The corn is turning brown;
The trees in apple orchards
  With fruit are bending down.

The gentian's bluest fringes
  Are curling in the sun;
In dusky pods the milkweed
  Its hidden silk has spun.

The sedges flaunt their harvest
  In every meadow nook,
And asters by the brookside
  Make asters in the brook.

From dewy lanes at morning
  The grape's sweet odours rise;
At noon the roads all flutter
  With golden butterflies.

By all these lovely tokens
  September days are here,
With summer's best of weather
  And autumn's best of cheer.

HELEN HUNT JACKSON

"ONE, TWO, THREE"

I<small>T</small> was an old, old, old, old lady
   And a boy that was half-past three,
And the way that they played together
   Was beautiful to see.

She couldn't go running and jumping,
   And the boy, no more could he;
For he was a thin little fellow,
   With a thin little twisted knee.

They sat in the yellow sunlight,
   Out under the maple tree,
And the game that they played I'll tell you,
   Just as it was told to me.

It was Hide-and-Go-Seek they were playing,
   Though you'd never have known it to be—
With an old, old, old, old lady
   And a boy with a twisted knee.

The boy would bend his face down
   On his little sound right knee,
And he'd guess where she was hiding,
   In guesses One, Two, Three.

" You are in the china closet? "
  He would cry and laugh with glee—
It wasn't the china closet—
  But he still had Two and Three.

"You are up in Papa's big bed-room,
  In the chest with the queer old key?"
And she said: "You are warm and warmer;
  But you're not quite right," said she.

"It can't be the little cupboard
  Where Mamma's things used to be—
So it must be the clothes-press, Grandma;"
  And he found her with his Three.

Then she covered her face with her fingers,
  That were wrinkled and white and wee,
And she guessed where the boy was hiding,
  With a One and a Two and a Three.

And they never had stirred from their places
  Right under the maple tree—
This old, old, old, old lady
  And the boy with the lame little knee—
This dear, dear, dear old lady
  And the boy who was half-past three.

H. C. BUNNER

ADVICE

THERE was once a pretty chicken,
But his friends were very few,
For he thought that there was nothing
In the world but what he knew.
So he always, in the farmyard,
Had a very forward way,
Telling all the hens and turkeys
What they ought to do and say.
"Mrs. Goose," he said, "I wonder
That your goslings you should let
Go out paddling in the water;
It will kill them to get wet.

" And I wish, my old Aunt Dorking,"
He began to her one day,
"That you wouldn't sit all summer
In your nest upon the hay;
Won't you come out to the meadow,
Where the grass with seeds is filled?"
" If I should," said Mrs. Dorking,
" Then my eggs would get all chilled."
" No, they won't," replied the chicken;
" And no matter if they do.
Eggs are really good for nothing.
What's an egg to me or you?"

"What's an egg?" said Mrs. Dorking,
"Can it be you do not know?
You, yourself, were in an egg-shell
Just a little month ago,—
And if kind wings had not warmed you,
You would not be out to-day,
Telling hens, and geese, and turkeys,
What they ought to do or say!"

To be very wise and show it,
Is a pleasant thing, no doubt;
But when young folks talk to old folks,
They should know what they're about.

THE BOY AND THE FILBERTS

A little boy once put his hand into a pitcher nearly filled with filberts.

He seized as many as his hand would hold. But when he tried to draw out his closed fist, he could not do so, as the neck of the pitcher was very narrow.

Not willing to lose the nuts he had grasped, he began to cry.

His mother gave him this wise advice: "Be satisfied with half the number of nuts, and your hand will come out with ease."

ÆSOP

SOMEBODY'S MOTHER

THE woman was old, and ragged, and gray,
And bent with the chill of the winter's day;

The street was wet with a recent snow,
And the woman's feet were aged and slow.

She stood at the crossing, and waited long,
Alone, uncared for, amid the throng

Of human beings who passed her by,
Nor heeded the glance of her anxious eye.

Down the street, with laughter and shout,
Glad in the freedom of " school let out,"

Came the boys, like a flock of sheep,
Hailing the snow, piled white and deep.

Past the woman so old and gray
Hastened the children on their way;

Nor offered a helping hand to her,
So meek, so timid, afraid to stir,

Lest the carriage wheels or the horses' feet
Should knock her down in the slippery street.

At last came one of the merry troop—
The gayest laddie of all the group;

He paused beside her and whispered low:
" I'll help you across if you wish to go."

Her aged hand on his strong young arm
She placed, and so, without hurt or harm,

He guided the trembling feet along,
Proud that his own were firm and strong.

Then back to his friends again he went,
His young heart happy and well content.

"She's somebody's mother, boys, you know,
For all she's aged, and poor, and slow ;

"And I hope some fellow will lend a hand
To help my mother, you understand,

" If ever she's poor, and old, and gray,
When her own dear boy is far away."

And "somebody's mother" bowed low her head
In her home that night, and the prayer she said

Was, " God be kind to the noble boy,
Who is somebody's son, and pride, and joy."

UNKNOWN

THE RABBIT'S TRICK

ONE day Brother Rabbit was running along the sea-shore when he saw a Whale and an Elephant talking together. He crouched down and listened to what they were saying, and this is what he heard:

"You are the biggest animal on the land, Brother Elephant," said the Whale, "and I am the biggest one in the sea; if we work together, we can rule all the animals and do just as we please."

"Excellent," said the Elephant; "that just suits me; we'll do it."

The Rabbit smiled. "They will not rule me," he said. Off he ran and soon came back with a long strong rope and a big drum. He hid the drum some distance away in the bushes. Then he ran along the shore till he met the Whale.

"Brother Whale," said he, "will you do me a favour? My cow is stuck in the mud away back in the bushes, and I am not strong enough to pull her out. May I ask you to help me?"

"Certainly," said the Whale, "I shall be glad to assist you."

"Then," said the Rabbit, "let me tie this end of my rope round you, and I will run back into the bushes and tie the other end round my cow, and when I have done that, I will beat on my drum. You will have to pull hard, for the cow is down deep in the mud."

"Pshaw!" said the Whale, "I will pull her out even if she is covered to the tips of her horns."

The Rabbit tied the rope to the Whale and ran off as fast as he could to the place where the Elephant was feeding.

"Dear Mr. Elephant," said he, "will you do me a kindness?"

"What do you want?" asked the Elephant.

"My cow is stuck in the mud some distance down on the shore, and I am not strong enough to pull her out. May I ask you to help me?"

"Why, of course," said the Elephant.

"Then," said the Rabbit, "let me tie the end of this rope to your trunk and the other to my cow, and when I have done this, I will beat on my big drum. When you hear that, pull with all your might, for the cow is a large one."

"Nonsense," said the Elephant. "I could pull a dozen cows."

"I feel sure of that," said the Rabbit, "only do not pull too hard at first."

When he had tied the rope about the Elephant's trunk, he ran back to a little hill in the bushes, where he could see what was about to happen, and began to beat the drum.

Whale and Elephant began at once to pull.

"A remarkably heavy cow," said the Elephant, as he braced himself, "but out she must come."

"Well, well!" said the Whale, "that cow must be far down in the mud."

Hard as the Whale pulled, the Elephant pulled harder, for he had a more solid foot-

ing.   Presently the Whale found himself
sliding towards the shore.   As he neared
the land, he became so indignant at the
thought of that cow, that he plunged violent-
ly head foremost to the bottom.   This jerked
the Elephant off his feet, and before he could
recover himself, he was pulled right down to
the edge of the water.   He was furious.

Just then the Whale ceased pulling for an
instant, and the Elephant leaped back with
a jerk that brought the Whale to the sur-
face of the water.

"What do you suppose you are pulling
on?" shouted the Whale.

"What are you doing with that rope?"
roared the Elephant.

"I will teach you to play cow," said the
Elephant.

"And I will show you how to trick me,"
said the Whale.

Each put forth all his strength, but the
rope broke and heels over head tumbled
Elephant and Whale.   This made them

both so ashamed and angry that it broke up the bargain between them.

And that little Rabbit in the bushes declared that he had never had such fun in his life.

When we get married and the children come
Each day the pressure grows
That's when we should spend some time alone
And take time off to smell the rose.

INDIAN SUMMER

ALONG the line of smoky hills
   The crimson forest stands,
And all the day the blue-jay calls
   Throughout the autumn lands.

Now by the brook the maple leans
   With all his glory spread,
And all the sumacs on the hills
   Have turned their green to red.

Now by great marshes wrapped in mist,
   Or past some river's mouth,
Throughout the long, still autumn day
   Wild birds are flying south.

                  W. WILFRED CAMPBELL

———

A gentle spirit, and a heart
That's quick to understand;
With these in my small corner
May I spread joy and light
And take a friendly candle
Into someone else's lonely night.

THE DUEL

THE gingham dog and the calico cat
Side by side on the table sat ;
'Twas half-past twelve, and (what do you think !)
Nor one nor t'other had slept a wink !
The old Dutch clock and the Chinese plate
Appeared to know as sure as fate
There was going to be a terrible spat.
(I wasn't there; I simply state
What was told to me by the Chinese plate !)

The gingham dog went " bow-wow-wow ! "
And the calico cat replied " mee-ow ! "

The air was littered, an hour or so,
With bits of gingham and calico,
While the old Dutch clock in the chimney-place
Up with its hands before its face,
For it always dreaded a family row !
> (*Now mind : I'm only telling you*
> *What the old Dutch clock declares is true !*)

The Chinese plate looked very blue,
And wailed : " Oh, dear ! what shall we do ! "
But the gingham dog and the calico cat
Wallowed this way and tumbled that,
Employing every tooth and claw
In the awfullest way you ever saw—
And, oh ! how the gingham and calico flew !
> (*Don't fancy I exaggerate !*
> *I got my views from the Chinese plate !*)

Next morning where the two had sat
They found no trace of the dog or cat ;
And some folks think unto this day
That burglars stole the pair away !
But the truth about the cat and the pup
Is this : They ate each other up !
Now what do you really think of that !
> (*The old Dutch clock it told me so,*
> *And that is how I came to know.*)

EUGENE FIELD

LITTLE GUSTAVA

LITTLE Gustava sits in the sun,
Safe in the porch, and the little drops run
From the icicles under the eaves so fast,
For the bright spring sun shines warm at last,
   And glad is little Gustava.

She wears a quaint little scarlet cap,
And a little green bowl she holds in her lap,
Filled with bread and milk to the brim,
And a wreath of marigolds round the rim;
   " Ha, ha!" laughs little Gustava.

Up comes her little gray coaxing cat,
With her little pink nose, and she mews :
    " What's that ? "
Gustava feeds her—she begs for more ;
And a little brown hen walks in at the door ;
    " Good-day ! " cries little Gustava.

She scatters crumbs for the little brown hen ;
There comes a rush and a flutter, and then
Down fly her little white doves, so sweet,
With their snowy wings and their crimson
    feet ;
    " Welcome," cries little Gustava.

So dainty and eager, they pick up the crumbs.
But who is this through the doorway comes ?
Little Scotch terrier, little dog Rags
Looks in her face, and his funny tail wags ;
    " Ha, ha ! " laughs little Gustava.

" You want some breakfast, too ? " and down
She sets her bowl on the brick floor brown ;
And little dog Rags drinks up her milk,
While she strokes his shaggy locks like silk ;
    " Dear Rags ! " says little Gustava.

Waiting without, stood sparrow and crow,
Cooling their feet in the melting snow ;

" Won't you come in, good folk ? " she cried.
But they were too bashful, and stayed outside,
    Though " Pray come in ! " cried Gustava.

So the last she threw them, and knelt on the
       mat
With doves and biddy and dog and cat.
And her mother came to the open house door:
" Dear little daughter, I bring you some more,
    My merry little Gustava ! "

Kitty and terrier, biddy and doves,
All things harmless Gustava loves.
The shy, kind creatures 'tis joy to feed,
And oh, her breakfast is sweet indeed
    To happy little Gustava !

CELIA THAXTER

    IF I can stop one heart from breaking,
      I shall not live in vain ;
If I can ease one life the aching,
      Or cool one pain,
Or help one fainting robin
      Into his nest again,
I shall not live in vain.

EMILY DICKINSON

THE BLUEBIRD

I KNOW the song that the bluebird is singing
Out in the apple tree where he is swinging.
Brave little fellow! the skies may be dreary;
Nothing cares he while his heart is so cheery.

Hark! how the music leaps out from his
   throat;
Hark! was there ever so merry a note?
Listen awhile, and you'll hear what he's
   saying
Up in the apple trees, swinging and swaying:

"Dear little blossoms down under the snow,
You must be weary of winter, I know;
Hark! while I sing you a message of cheer,
Summer is coming, and spring-time is here!

"Little white snowdrop, I pray you, arise;
Bright yellow crocus, come, open your eyes;
Sweet little violets, hid from the cold,
Put on your mantles of purple and gold;
Daffodils! daffodils! say, do you hear?
Summer is coming, and spring-time is here!"

EMILY HUNTINGTON MILLER

MOTHER PARTRIDGE

Down the wooded slope of Taylor's Hill
Mother Partridge led her brood; down
toward the crystal brook that by some
strange whim was called Mud Creek.   Her
little ones were one day old, but already
quick on foot, and she was taking them for
the first time to drink.

She walked slowly, crouching low as she
went, for the woods were full of enemies.
She was uttering a soft little cluck in her
throat, a call to the little balls of mottled
down that on their tiny pink legs came
toddling after, and peeping softly and plain-
tively if left even a few inches behind, and
seeming so fragile they made the very chick-
adees look big and coarse.

There were twelve of them, but Mother
Partridge watched them all, and she watched
every bush and tree and thicket, and the
whole woods, and the sky itself.   Always for
enemies she seemed seeking—friends were
too scarce to be looked for—and an enemy

she found. Away across the level beaver meadow was a great brute of a fox. He was coming their way, and in a few moments would surely wind them, or strike their trail. There was no time to lose.

"Krrr! Krrr!" (Hide! Hide!) cried the mother in a low firm voice, and the little bits of things, scarcely bigger than acorns and but a day old, scattered far (a few inches) apart to hide. One dived under a leaf, another between two roots, a third crawled into a curl of birch-bark, a fourth into a hole, and so on till all were hidden but one who could find no cover, so squatted on a broad yellow chip and lay very flat, and closed his eyes very tight, sure that now he was safe from being seen. They ceased their frightened peeping, and all was still.

Mother Partridge flew straight towards the dreaded beast, alighted fearlessly a few yards to one side of him, and then flung herself on the ground, flopping as though winged and lame—oh, so dreadfully lame—

and whining like a distressed puppy. Was she begging for mercy—mercy from a bloodthirsty, cruel fox? Oh, dear no! She was no fool. One often hears of the cunning of the fox. Wait and see what a fool he is compared with a mother-partridge. Elated at the prize so suddenly within his reach, the fox turned with a dash and caught—at least, no, he didn't quite catch the bird; she flopped, by chance, just a foot out of reach. He followed with another jump and would have seized her this time surely, but somehow a sapling came just between, and the partridge dragged herself awkwardly away and under a log; but the great brute snapped his jaws and bounded over the log, while she, seeming a trifle less lame, made another clumsy forward spring and tumbled down a bank, and Reynard, keenly following, almost caught her tail, but, oddly enough, fast as he went and leaped, she still seemed just a trifle faster. It was most extraordinary. A winged partridge and he, Reynard, the Swift-foot, had not caught her in five minutes' racing. It was really shameful. But the partridge seemed to gain strength as the fox put forth his, and after a quarter of a mile race, racing that was somehow all away from Taylor's Hill, the bird got unaccountably quite well, and, rising with a derisive whirr, flew off through the woods, leaving the fox, utterly dumfounded, to realize that he had been made a fool of, and, worst of all, he now remembered that this was not the first time he had been served this very trick, though he never knew the reason for it.

Meanwhile Mother Partridge skimmed in a great circle, and came by a roundabout way back to the little fuzzballs she had left hidden in the woods.

ERNEST THOMPSON-SETON
"Wild Animals I Have Known"

A SONG

If there is laughter in your heart
Don't hold it for to-morrow,
Let us sing for all our worth
Nor give a thought for sorrow,
None knows what lies along the way;
Let's smile what smiles we can to-day.

EGAR GUEST

LISTEN TO THE RAIN

Listen to the Rain!
Hear the merry sound it makes
As it falls and slides and shakes
From the eaves into the street,
Where its million tiny feet
Hurry, hurry past the door,
Followed by a million more!

Listen to the Rain!
How it gurgles with delight,
Hurling from its dizzy height,

Falling straight and falling true,
Faster now, and louder, too —
See!   The tardy drops and small
Cannot keep the pace at all!

Listen to the Rain!
Ah!   It's angry now — I fear
'Tis a scolding voice you hear!
How it scolds the drooping trees,
How it scolds the languid breeze,
How it scolds the birds, poor things,
For the dust upon their wings!

Listen to the Rain!
If you listen hard, you'll hear
How the skies grow cool and clear,
How the primrose lifts her head,
How the mountain brooks are fed,
How the earth grows sweet again
With the coming of the Rain!

ISABEL ECCLESTONE MACKAY

IF a thought comes quick of doing a kindness
to a friend, do it that very moment! Don't
put it off—don't wait.   What's the use of
doing a kindness, if you do it a day too late.

CHARLES KINGSLEY

THEY DIDN'T THINK

Once a trap was baited
  With a piece of cheese;
It smelled so strong to mousie,
  It almost made him sneeze.
An old mouse said: "There's danger;
  Be careful where you go!"
"Nonsense," replied the other;
  "I don't believe you know!"

So he walked in boldly,
  No one was in sight;
First he took a nibble,
  Then he took a bite.
Close the trap together
  Snapped, as quick as wink,

Catching little mousie there,
   Because he " didn't think."

Once a little robin
   Stood outside the door;
He wanted to go inside,
   And hop upon the floor.
" No, no," said the mother,
   " You must stay with me;
Little birds are safest
   Sitting in a tree!"

" I don't care," said Robin,
   And gave his tail a fling;
" I believe you old folks
   Don't know everything."
He went; but Pussy seized him,
   Before he'd time to blink.
" Oh," he cried : " I'm sorry !
   But I didn't think."

Now, my little children,
   Learn from this my song,
Young folks are not always right,
   Nor old folks always wrong.
Don't suppose you know more
   Than anybody knows;
For there's often danger
   Where no danger shows.

A VISIT FROM ST. NICHOLAS

'Twas the night before Christmas, when all
    through the house
Not a creature was stirring, not even a mouse;
The stockings were hung by the chimney with
    care,
In hopes that St. Nicholas soon would be there;
The children were nestled all snug in their beds,
While visions of sugar-plums danced in their
    heads;

And mamma in her kerchief, and I in my cap,
Had just settled our brains for a long winter's
    nap,—
When out on the lawn there arose such a clatter,
I sprang from my bed to see what was the
    matter.

Away to the window I flew like a flash,
Tore open the shutters, and threw up the sash.
The moon on the breast of the new-fallen snow
Gave a lustre of mid-day to objects below
When what to my wondering eyes should appear
But a miniature sleigh, and eight tiny reindeer.
With a little old driver, so lively and quick,
I knew in a moment it must be St. Nick.

More rapid than eagles his coursers they came,
And he whistled and shouted, and called them
    by name:
"Now, Dasher! now, Dancer! now, Prancer
    and Vixen!
On, Comet! on, Cupid! on, Donder and Blitzen!
To the top of the porch! to the top of the wall!
Now dash away! dash away! dash away, all!"
As dry leaves that before the wild hurricane fly,
When they meet with an obstacle, mount to the
    sky,

So up to the housetop the coursers they flew
With the sleigh full of toys,—and St. Nicholas,
   too.

And then in a twinkling I heard on the roof
The prancing and pawing of each little hoof;
As I drew in my head, and was turning around,
Down the chimney St. Nicholas came with a
   bound.
He was dressed all in fur from his head to his
   foot,
And his clothes were all tarnished with ashes
   and soot;
A bundle of toys he had flung on his back,
And he looked like a pedlar just opening his
   pack.
His eyes—how they twinkled! his dimples—
   how merry!
His cheeks were like roses, his nose like a
   cherry!

His droll little mouth was drawn up like a bow,
And the beard of his chin was as white as the
   snow;
The stump of a pipe he held tight in his teeth,
And the smoke it encircled his head like a
   wreath.

He had a broad face, and a little round belly
That shook when he laughed like a bowl full of
jelly.
He was chubby and plump,—a right jolly old
elf,—
And I laughed, when I saw him, in spite of
myself.

A wink of his eye and a twist of his head
Soon gave me to know I had nothing to dread.
He spoke not a word, but went straight to his
work
And filled all the stockings ; then turned with
a jerk,
And laying his finger aside of his nose,
And giving a nod, up the chimney he rose.
He sprang to his sleigh, to his team gave a
whistle,
And away they all flew like the down of a
thistle.
But I heard him exclaim, ere he drew out of
sight,
" Happy Christmas to all ! and to all a good-
night ! "

CLEMENT C. MOORE

THE DARING FROGGIE

Once upon a time,
　　On the border of a brook,
A wicked little froggie,
　　Who had never read a book—
Who had never read a story,
　　Or a funny little rhyme,
Had a sad and tragic ending,
　　Once upon a time.

The little froggie, sad to say,
　　Was very fond of flies,
And thought, on this unlucky day,
　　That he had found a prize.

"Up, up, I go," said Froggie,
 "I can climb as well as hop;
I only hope he'll stay right there
  Until I reach the top.

"I wish this wouldn't bend so much,"
  Said Froggie, going higher;
"I wish that flies would shut their
    eyes,
  And come a little nigher.
But he is such a good one,
  And he looks so very fine,
I think that I must have him,
  For it's time for me to dine."

So up he went, regardless
  Of the danger he was in;
He saw a duck below him,
  But he didn't care a pin;
Till suddenly, behind his back,
  The reed began to crack,
And all he heard was just one word,
  And that one word was "QUACK!"
                    JAMES CLARENCE HAWER

A little neglect may breed great mischief.
For want of a nail the shoe was lost; for
want of a shoe the horse was lost; and for
want of a horse the rider was lost.

THE CHILDREN'S HOUR

BETWEEN the dark and the daylight,
   When the night is beginning to lower,
Comes a pause in the day's occupations,
   That is known as the children's hour.

I hear in the chamber above me
   The patter of little feet,
The sound of a door that is opened,
   And voices soft and sweet.

From my study I see in the lamplight,
    Descending the broad hall stair,
Grave Alice, and laughing Allegra,
    And Edith with golden hair.

A whisper, and then a silence:
    Yet I know by their merry eyes
They are plotting and planning together
    To take me by surprise.

A sudden rush from the stairway,
    A sudden raid from the hall!
By three doors left unguarded
    They enter my castle wall!

They climb up into my turret
    O'er the arms and back of my chair;
If I try to escape, they surround me;
    They seem to be everywhere.

They almost devour me with kisses,
    Their arms about me entwine,
Till I think of the Bishop of Bingen
    In his Mouse-Tower on the Rhine!

Do you think, O blue-eyed banditti,
    Because you have scaled the wall,
Such an old moustache as I am
    Is not a match for you all!

I have you fast in my fortress,
   And will not let you depart,
But put you down into the dungeon
   In the round-tower of my heart.

And there will I keep you for ever,
   Yes, for ever and a day,
Till the walls shall crumble to ruin,
   And moulder in dust away!

LONGFELLOW

A WISH

I'd like to be a boy again, a carefree prince of joy again
I'd like to tread the hills and dales the way I used to do;
I'd like the tattered shirt again, the knickers thick with
dirt again
The ugly dusty feet that long ago I knew.

I'd like to play first base again and Sliver's curves to
face again
I'd like to climb the way I did a friendly apple tree;
For knowing what I do today, could I but wander back
and play
To get full measure of the joy, that boyhood gave to me.

GUEST

SORRY DAD

I'm sorry dad but I'm just a lad
And I didn't mean it to happen this way,
My foot made a slip and the ball took a flip
And the T.V. got in the way.

Do you remember dad, when you were a lad
The window pane you broke in the old rural school,
The teacher didn't make a noise, "Oh boys will be boys,"
So daddy please keep your cool.

I'll run like the dickens and feed all the chickens
To make up for the way I blew it,
I'll go get the cows and slop the sows
Because daddy I really didn't mean to do it.

Some day I may own, a farm of my own
And have a little son to brighten my load,
So daddy please-be-kind, then I think you'll find
I'll be good to your grandson somewhere down the road.

MDF

I'M COMING DAD

I'm coming dad please wait for me
My legs are a little short you see
Give me a lift when the going's rough
And when I'm bad don't be tough

I'm coming dad a little faster now
It won't be long till I show you how
When I get to be five or six
I'll show you all the new tricks

I'm coming dad along through school
So I won't be a silly fool
And if we're lucky you might be
More than a little proud of me

Now I must go to do my thing
What ever fame or fortune it might bring
To sing my song, to seek my wife
To rise or fall, to live my life.

Now hurry dad, you're getting slow
Silver in your hair now starts to show
I listen patiently as your stories you repeat
Your tales come from your favourite seat.

I'm coming son please wait for me
It seems I have an artificial knee
Give me a hand through the ice and snow
I waited for you just a few years ago.

BERNIE HANN
DELAWARE

Love and joy is Valentine's Day
Children smiling from ear to ear
Wouldn't it be nice if Valentine's Day
Was every day of the year.

REMINISCING

I've lived many dreams that never came true
I've seen them banish at dawn,
But I've realized enough of my dreams
To make me want to dream on.

I've prayed many prayers - when no answer came
Though I waited patiently and long,
But answers have come to enough of my prayers
To make me want to pray on.

I've trusted many a friend - who failed!
And left me to weep alone,
But I've found enough of my friends true blue
To make me want to trust on.

I've drained the cup of disappointment and pain
And gone many a day without a song,
But I've sipped enough nectar from the roses of life
To make me want to live on.

Sieka Van Steeg
Poplar Hill

LITTLE BATEESE

You're a bad little boy, not much you care
How busy you're keeping your old grand'pere
Trying to stop you every day
From chasing the hens around the hay.
Why don't you give them a chance to lay
Little Bateese.

But Little Bateese, please don't forget
We would rather you would stay a small boy yet
So chase the chickens and give them a scare
And do what you like with your old grand'pere
For when you're a big feller I won't be there
Little Bateese.

SKIPPY

You little dog "Skippy" you're so happy and gay
You never stay still one minute of the day
Chasing a ball or the old tom cat,
Snitching and taking off with the little boy's hat.
You welcome me back when I come home each night
And the show you put on is really a sight
Till I fondly scold you "get down you pup
Are you so glad that you would eat me up?"
She's the truest little friend I ever had
If she wasn't here to greet me I'd be mighty sad.

BUD

Who is it who lives to the full every minute
Gets all the joy and fun that is in it?
Tough as they make them and ready to race,
Fit for a battle and fit for a chase
Heedless of buttons on blouses and pants
Laughing at danger and taking a chance,
Gladdest it seems when he wallows in mud
Who is the rascal? I'll tell you its Bud!

Who is reckless of stocking and heedless of shoes?
Who laughs at a tumble and grins at a bruise?
Who climbs over fences and clambers up trees
And scrapes all the skin off his shins and his knees?
Who is prince to his mother and king to his dad
And makes us forget that we ever were sad?
Who is center of all that we dream of and plan
Our baby to-day but to-morrow our man?
Its that tough little, rough little tyke in the mud
That tousled-haired, fun loving rascal called Bud.

THE RAG DOLL

There's the flaxen haired doll with the real human hair.
There's the teddy bear left all alone,
There's the automobile at the foot of the stair.
And there's her little toy telephone;
We thought they were fine but a little child's eyes
Look deeper than ours to find charm.
And now she's in bed and the rag dolly lies
Cuddled close on her little white arm.

EDGAR GUEST

THE BROOK

I COME from haunts of coot and hern,
  I make a sudden sally,
And sparkle out among the fern,
  To bicker down a valley.

I chatter, chatter, as I flow
  To join the brimming river,
For men may come and men may go,
  But I go on for ever.

I wind about, and in and out,
  With here a blossom sailing,
And here and there a lusty trout,
  And here and there a grayling,

And here and there a foamy flake
  Upon me, as I travel
With many a silvery waterbreak
  Above the golden gravel,

And draw them all along, and flow
  To join the brimming river,
For men may come and men may go,
  But I go on for ever.

I steal by lawns and grassy plots,
  I slide by hazel covers;
I move the sweet forget-me-nots
  That grow for happy lovers.

I slip, I slide, I gloom, I glance,
   Among my skimming swallows;
I make the netted sunbeam dance
   Against my sandy shallows.

I murmur under moon and stars
   In brambly wildernesses;
I linger by my shingly bars;
   I loiter round my cresses;

And out again I curve and flow
   To join the brimming river,
For men may come and men may go,
   But I go on for ever.   Tennyson

If you meet a person without a smile
This is one of the greatest cures,
Look that person straight in the eye
And give them one of yours.

If you have love to give and share,
Don t hide your love away,
But let it shine like morning sun
To cheer a cloudy day.

May the wind bring to the shores of your life
The happiness created by contentment and peace,
And may the troubles that torture our mind
Through the sweet things of life forever cease.

MDF

He prayeth best who loveth best
All things both great and small;
For the dear God who loveth us,
He made and loveth all.

Coleridge

ABIDE WITH ME

ABIDE with me! fast falls the eventide;
The darkness deepens; LORD with me abide!
When other helpers fail, and comforts flee,
Help of the helpless, O abide with me!

Swift to its close ebbs out life's little day;
Earth's joys grow dim, its glories pass away;
Change and decay in all around I see;
O Thou who changest not, abide with me!

I need Thy Presence every passing hour:
What but Thy grace can foil the tempter's
   power?
Who like Thyself my guide and stay can be?
Through cloud and sunshine, O abide with me!

I fear no foe with Thee at hand to bless;
Ills have no weight and tears no bitterness.
Where is death's sting? where, Grave, thy
   victory?
I triumph still if Thou abide with me!

                      HENRY FRANCIS LYTE

Sketch by Ron Nickles

LOBO SS #3
SCHOOL BUILT IN 1870

It's nice to see, S.S. No. 3
Sweet memories come drifting back,
We rolled in the clover, played anti, I over
And ate lunch on the woodpile at the back.

The one room took care, of thirty of us there
From the little ones right up to grade eight,
We learned to share, and we learned to care
And we learned to play the game straight.

Some chums are gone but we carry on
Each day with many a backward look,
And now my friend, this is the end
And I hope you enjoyed our book.

TILL WE MEET AGAIN
MASON